De
Profundis

De
Profundis

Oscar Wilde

This edition published in 2019 by Arcturus Publishing Limited
26/27 Bickels Yard, 151–153 Bermondsey Street,
London SE1 3HA

AD006595UK

Printed in the UK

Contents

❦Introduction

Oscar Wilde's *De Profundis* is an extraordinary love letter. Not only is it exceptionally long but also, perhaps surprisingly, quite universal: the rawness, pain and contradictions of an intense yet intrinsically damaged and damaging love affair resonate throughout humankind. As a result, it offers readers a fascinating insight into the specifics of time and culture that led an acclaimed playwright to a tangled decline.

Known primarily as a playwright and poet, Wilde was born into an Anglo-Irish family in Dublin on 16 October 1854. His parents were intellectuals: his father a surgeon, his mother a poet, both with wide-ranging interests. The young Oscar did well at his studies, showing a talent for languages (he learned French and German fluently), and went on to study classics at Trinity College, Dublin and then at Magdalen College, Oxford; he won scholarships to both, and literary prizes for his poetry. He was drawn, too, to philosophise on the nature of art and creativity, championing the aesthetic movement of John Ruskin and Walter Pater. Matching his ideas with flamboyant, languid surroundings and lifestyle, clothed in velvet and silk, he was famed for his witty epigrams as much as for his literary work.

In his thirties, Wilde turned to journalism, and was editor

Introduction

of *The Woman's World* from 1887 to 1889. After that he moved into fiction, publishing his only full-length novel, *The Picture of Dorian Gray*, in 1890–1. His best-loved works, the polished comedy dramas *Lady Windermere's Fan*, *A Woman of No Importance*, *The Ideal Husband* and *The Importance of Being Earnest*, followed in the early to mid 1890s, and it was these that established for him a new standing in society. They combine amusing social frippery with incisively observant detail of human behaviour; *The Importance of Being Earnest* especially was the source of many a witticism that has passed into the English language, among them: 'To lose one parent, Mr Worthing, may be regarded as a misfortune; to lose both looks like carelessness.'

Wilde's personal life, however, would lead him in a different direction. In 1884 he married Constance Lloyd, with whom he set up home for the next decade in Tite Street, in London's Chelsea. The couple had two sons, Cyril and Vyvyan, who were immensely important to Wilde. But ultimately neither heterosexuality nor quiet domesticity were enough for him, and he increasingly pursued reckless pleasures and began to embark on homosexual liaisons – at first primarily romantic, then in later years physical too. In 1891 he met Lord Alfred Douglas, known as Bosie, a feckless and spoilt but handsome young Oxford undergraduate, 16 years Wilde's junior. Endlessly exploited by Douglas, but unable to resist, Wilde fell into a complex relationship that would dictate the course

of the rest of his life. Douglas introduced him to the under-world of gay prostitution, and clocked up massive gambling and dining debts on Wilde's tab.

The situation came to a head in 1894, when Douglas's father, the Marquess of Queensberry, objected vociferously and publicly to his son's relationship with Wilde. By 1895, Wilde – egged on by Douglas, who harboured an obsessive, point-scoring hatred for his father – was suing Queensberry for criminal libel over the accusations of sodomy. Wilde, according to his account in *De Profundis*, expected the trial to focus on his letters to Douglas, which he explained away as art, but Queensberry had hired private detectives and tracked down underworld contacts who told of a lurid life-style that shocked society. The tide of the trial quickly turned against Wilde, who dropped the charges. However, he was bankrupted by having to pay Queensberry's legal expenses and, to make matters worse, he was soon on trial himself, for 'gross indecency'. At first his eloquence protected him, and the jury could not agree on a verdict; but after a retrial he was convicted and sentenced to two years' hard labour.

Most of that incarceration took place in Reading Gaol, and it was there, when he was eventually allowed pen and paper, that Wilde wrote *De Profundis*. The letter is presented as his explanation of events, supposedly for Douglas' benefit but unarguably more recrimination than gift. Wilde has no illusions about his own self-destructive weakness (in contrast

to his far-from-modest opinion of his literary talent): time and again he tries to walk away from Douglas, only to be drawn back. He rails against his young lover for disrupting his ability to work and for leaving him bankrupt – and being unconcerned by both facts – yet although he cannot admit it, he knows the self-indulgent youth is incapable of understanding. He scorns the boy's literary efforts, and himself for stooping so low as to beg for minuscule crumbs of love. Douglas emerges as self-absorbed and emotionally immature, without a shred of human kindness, and beset by a deeply dysfunctional family; Wilde's humiliation is vast and painful to read, but it comes over as essentially an extreme version of a blend of self-delusion and clear-sightedness that can form part of many healthier relationships.

The later part of the letter focuses on other themes. Wilde spends many pages discussing his views on Christianity, with a fascinating take that treats Christ as an artist and His views as artistic structures. He also writes of the experience of being in prison, its potential for spiritual redemption, and the need for love and a generosity of spirit as a means to survive: 'At all costs I must keep Love in my heart. If I go into prison without Love, what will become of my soul?' The letter was clearly cathartic for Wilde in many ways. It was not sent, but he was allowed to keep it.

After those two long years, Wilde was released from prison in May 1897. He was in a sorry state, crippled by

Introduction

bankruptcy as much as by the destructive hardships of incarceration and emotional abandonment. Not only had Douglas ignored him the whole time he was in prison in Reading, but he was now estranged from his wife and denied access to his beloved sons. Supported by a loyal handful of friends, he managed to leave Britain for France. There he eventually achieved a reconciliation of sorts with Douglas, and wrote 'The Ballad of Reading Gaol', a poem about the inhumane, brutal conditions suffered by prison inmates, told through the story of a man he had known in Reading. But he never really recovered from the ordeal, and died suddenly of meningitis in Paris on 25 November 1900, aged 46. He is buried in the Père Lachaise cemetery there.

Today, Wilde is remembered equally for his sensational love affair and imprisonment as for his enduring, polished plays that coax us into laughing while wincing at society's foibles. *De Profundis* reveals much of the man behind it all. Unlike many of its predecessors (some of which removed all references to Douglas), this edition is published in its entirety, unabridged. Meaning 'from the depths' in Latin, the title is taken from the start of Psalm 130: 'Out of the depths have I cried unto thee, O Lord.'

De Profundis

Dear Bosie,

After long and fruitless waiting I have determined to write
to you myself, as much for your sake as for mine, as I would
not like to think that I had passed through two long years
of imprisonment without even having received a single line
from you, or any news or message even, except such as gave
me pain.

Our ill fated and most lamentable friendship has ended
in ruin and public infamy for me, yet the memory of our
ancient affection is often with me, and the thought that
loathing, bitterness and contempt should for ever take that
place in my heart once held by love is very sad to me: and
you yourself will, I think, feel in your heart that to write to
me as I lie in the loneliness of prison-life is better than to
publish my letters without my permission or to dedicate
poems to me unasked, though the world will know nothing
of whatever words of grief or passion, or remorse or indifference you may choose to send as your answer or your
appeal.

I have no doubt that in this letter which I have to write
of your life and of mine, of the past and of the future, of
sweet things changed to bitterness and of bitter things that
may be turned to joy, there will be much that will wound
your vanity to the quick. If it prove so, read the letter over

and over again till it kills your vanity. If you find in it something of which you feel that you are unjustly accused, remember that one should be thankful that there is any fault of which one can be unjustly accused. If there be in it one single passage that brings tears to your eyes, weep as we weep in prison where the day no less than the night is set apart for tears. It is the only thing that can save you. If you go complaining to your mother, as you did with reference to the scorn of you I displayed in my letter to Robbie, so that she may flatter and soothe you back into self-complacency or conceit, you will be completely lost. If you find one false excuse for yourself, you will soon find a hundred, and be just what you were before. Do you still say, as you said to Robbie in your answer, that I *'attribute unworthy motives'* to you? Ah! You had no motives in life. You had appetites merely. A motive is an intellectual aim. That you were *'very young'* when our friendship began? Your defect was not that you knew so little about life, but that you knew so much. The morning dawn of boyhood with its delicate bloom, its clear pure light, its joy of innocence and expectation you had left far behind. With very swift and running feet you had passed from Romance to Realism. The gutter and the things that live in it had begun to fascinate you. That was the origin of the trouble in which you sought my aid, and I, so unwisely according to the wisdom of this world, out of pity and kindness gave it to you. You must read this letter

right through, though each word may become to you as the fire or knife of the surgeon that makes the delicate flesh burn or bleed. Remember that the fool in the eyes of the gods and the fool in the eyes of man are very different. One who is entirely ignorant of the modes of art in its revolution or the moods of thought in its progress, of the pomp of the Latin line or the richer music of the vowelled Greek, of Tuscan sculpture or Elizabethan song may yet be full of the very sweetest wisdom. The real fool, such as the gods mock or mar, is he who does not know himself. I was such a one too long. You have been such a one too long. Be so no more. Do not be afraid. The supreme vice is shallowness. Everything that is realised is right. Remember also that whatever is misery to you to read, is still greater misery to me to set down. To you the Unseen Powers have been very good. They have permitted you to see the strange and tragic shapes of life as one sees shadows in a crystal. The head of Medusa that turns living men to stone, you have been allowed to look at in a mirror merely. You yourself have walked free among the flowers. From me the beautiful world of colour and motion has been taken away.

I will begin by telling you that I blame myself terribly. As I sit here in this dark cell in convict clothes, a disgraced and ruined man, I blame myself. In the perturbed and fitful nights of anguish, in the long monotonous days of pain, it is myself I blame. I blame myself for allowing an unintel-

lectual friendship, a friendship whose primary aim was not the creation and contemplation of beautiful things, to entirely dominate my life. From the very first there was too wide a gap between us. You had been idle at your school, worse than idle at your University. You did not realise that an artist, and especially such an artist as I am, one, that is to say, the quality of whose work depends on the intensification of personality, requires for the development of his art the companionship of ideas, an intellectual atmosphere, quiet, peace, and solitude. You admired my work when it was finished: you enjoyed the brilliant successes of my first nights, and the brilliant banquets that followed them: you were proud, and quite naturally so, of being the intimate friend of an artist so distinguished; but you could not understand the conditions requisite for the production of artistic work. I am not speaking in phrases of rhetorical exaggeration but in terms of absolute truth to actual fact when I remind you that during the whole time we were together I never wrote one single line. Whether at Torquay, Goring, London, Florence or elsewhere, my life, as long as you were by my side, was entirely sterile and uncreative. And with but few intervals you were, I regret today, by my side always.

I remember, for instance, in September '93, to select merely one instance out of many, taking a set of chambers, purely in order to work undisturbed, as I had broken my contract with John Hare for whom I had promised to write

a play, and who was pressing me on the subject. During the first week you kept away. We had, not unnaturally indeed, differed on the question of the artistic value of your translation of *Salomé*, so you contented yourself with sending me foolish letters on the subject. In that week I wrote and completed in every detail, as it was ultimately performed, the first act of *An Ideal Husband*. The second week you returned and my week practically had to be given up. I arrived at St. James's Place every morning at 11.30, in order to have the opportunity of thinking and writing without the interruptions inseparable from my own house-hold, quiet and peaceful as that household was. But the attempt was vain. At 12 oc. [o'clock] you drove up, and stayed smoking cigarettes and chattering till 1.30, when I had to take you out to luncheon at the *Café Royal* in the Berkeley. Luncheon with its *liqueurs* lasted usually till 3.30. For an hour you retired to White's. At tea-time you appeared again, and stayed till it was time to dress for dinner. You dined with me either at the Savoy or at Tite Street. We did not separate as a rule till after midnight, as supper at Willis's had to wind up the entrancing day. That was my life for those three months, every single day, except during the four days when you went abroad. I then, of course, had to go over to Calais to fetch you back. For one of my nature and temperament it was a position at once grotesque and tragic.

You surely must realise that now? You must see now that your incapacity of being alone: your nature so exigent in its persistent claim on the attention and time of others: your lack of any power of sustained intellectual concentration: the unfortunate accident – for I like to think it was no more – that you had not yet been able to acquire the 'Oxford temper' in intellectual matters, never, I mean, been one who could play gracefully with ideas but had arrived at violence of opinion merely: – that all these things, combined with the fact that your desires and interests were in life not in art, were as destructive to your own progress in culture as they were to my work as an artist? When I compare my friendship with you to my friendship with such still younger men as John Gray and Pierre Louys I feel ashamed. My real life, my higher life was with them and such as they.

Of the appalling secrets of my friendship with you I don't speak at present. I am thinking merely of its quality while it lasted. It was intellectually degrading to me. You had the rudiments of an artistic temperament in its germ. But I met you either too late or too soon, I don't know which. When you were away I was all right. The moment, in the early December of the year to which I have been alluding, I had succeeded in inducing your mother to send you out of England, I collected again the torn and ravelled web of my imagination, got my life back into my own hands, and not merely finished the three remaining acts of the 'Ideal

De Profundis

Husband', but conceived and had almost completed two other plays of a completely different type, the 'Florentine Tragedy' and 'La Sainte Courtisane', when suddenly, unbidden, unwelcome, and under circumstances fatal to my happiness you returned. The two works left then imperfect I was unable to take up again. The mood that created them I could never recover. You now, having yourself published a volume of verse, will be able to recognise the truth of everything I have said here. Whether you can or not it remains as a hideous truth in the very heart of our friendship. While you were with me you were the absolute ruin of my art, and in allowing you to stand persistently between art and myself I give to myself shame and blame in the fullest degree. You couldn't know, you couldn't understand, you couldn't appreciate. I had no right to expect it of you at all. Your interests were merely in your meals and moods. Your desires were simply for amusements, for ordinary or less ordinary pleasures. They were what your temperament needed, or thought it needed for the moment. I should have forbidden you my house and my chambers except when I specially invited you. I blame myself without reserve for my weakness. It was merely weakness. One half hour with art was always more to me than a cycle with you. Nothing really at any period of my life was ever of the smallest importance to me compared with art. But in the case of an artist, weakness is nothing less than a crime, when it is a weakness that paralyses the imagination.

I blame myself again for having allowed you to bring me to utter and discreditable financial ruin. I remember one morning in the early October of '92 sitting in the yellowing woods at Bracknell with your mother. At that time I knew very little of your real nature. I had stayed from a Saturday to Monday with you at Oxford. You had stayed with me at Cromer for ten days and played golf. The conversation turned on you, and your mother began to speak to me about your character. She told me of your two chief faults, your vanity, and your being, as she termed it, *'all wrong about money.'* I had no idea that the first would bring me to prison, and the second to bankruptcy. I thought vanity a sort of graceful flower for a young man to wear, as for extravagance – for I thought she meant no more than extravagance – the virtues of prudence and thrift were not in my own nature or my own race. But before our friendship was one month older I began to see what your mother really meant. Your insistence on a life of reckless profusion: your incessant demands for money: your claim that all your pleasures should be paid for by me whether I was with you or not: brought me after some time into serious monetary difficulties, and what made the extravagances to me at any rate so monotously uninter-esting, as your persistent grasp on my life grew stronger and shorter, was that the money was really spent on little more than the pleasures of eating, drinking, and the like. Now and then it is a joy to have one's table red with wine and

roses, but you outstripped all taste and temperance. You demanded without grace and received without thanks. You grew to think that you had a sort of right to live at my expense and in a profuse luxury to which you had never been accustomed, and which for that reason made your appetites all the more keen, and at the end if you lost money gambling in some Algiers Casino you simply telegraphed next morning to me in London to lodge the amount of your losses to your account at your Bank, and gave the matter no further thought of any kind.

When I tell you that between the autumn of 1892 and the date of my imprisonment I spent with you and on you more than £5000 in actual money, irrespective of the bills I incurred, you will have some idea of the sort of life on which you insisted. Do you think I exaggerate? My ordinary expenses with you for an ordinary day in London – for luncheon, dinner, supper, arrangements, hansoms and the rest of it – ranged from £12 to £20, and the weeks expenses were naturally in proportion and ranged from £80 to £130. For our three months at Goring my expenses, (rent of course included) were £1340, step by step with the Bankruptcy-Receiver I had to go over every item of my life. It was horrible. '*Plain living and high thinking*' was, of course, an ideal you could not at that time have appreciated, but such extravagance was a disgrace to both of us. One of the most delightful dinners I remember ever having had is one Robbie

and I had together in a little Soho *café*, which cost about as many shillings as my dinners to you used to cost pounds. Out of my dinner with Robbie came the first and best of all my dialogues. Idea, title, entreatment, mode, everything was struck out at a 3 franc 50 c. *table-d'hôte*. Out of the reckless dinners with you nothing remains but the memory that too much was eaten and too much was drunk. And my yielding to your demands was bad for you. You know that now. It made you grasping often: at times not a little unscrupulous; ungracious always. There was on far too many occasions too little joy of privilege in being your host. You forgot – I will not say the formal courtesies of thanks, for formal courtesies will strain a close friendship – but simply the grace of sweet companionship, the charm of pleasant conversation, that τερπνον κακον as the Greeks called it, and all those gentle humanities that make life lovely and are an accompaniment to life as music might be, keeping things in tune and filling with melody the harsh or silent places. And though it may seem strange to you that one in the terrible position in which I am situated should find a difference between one disgrace and another, still I frankly admit that the folly of throwing away all this money on you, and letting you squander my fortune to your own hurt as well as to mine, gives to me and in my eyes a note of common profligacy to my Bankruptcy that makes me doubly ashamed of it. I was made for other things.

De Profundis

But most of all I blame myself in the entire ethical degradation I allowed you to bring on me. The basis of character is will-power, and my will-power became absolutely subject to yours. It sounds a grotesque thing to say, but it is none the less true. Those incessant scenes that seemed to be almost physically necessary to you, and in which your mind and body grew distorted and you became a thing as terrible to look at as to listen to: that dreadful mania you inherit from your father, the mania for writing revolting and loathsome letters: your entire lack of any control over your emotions as displayed in your long resentful moods of sullen silence, no less than in the sudden fits of almost epileptic rage: all these things in reference to which one of my letters to you, left by you laying about at the Savoy or some other Hotel and so produced in Court by your father's counsel, contained an entreaty not devoid of pathos, had you at that time been able to recognise pathos either in its elements or its expression: – These, I say, were the origin and causes of my fatal yielding to you in your daily increasing demands. You wore one out. It was the triumph of the smaller over the bigger nature. It was the case of that tyranny of the weak over the strong which somewhere in one of my plays I describe as being 'the only tyranny that lasts'. And it was inevitable. In every relation of life with others one has to find some *moyen de vivre*. In your case, one has either to give up to you or to give you up. There was no other alternative. Through deep if misplaced

afffection for you: through great pity for your defects of temper and temperament: through my own proverbial good-nature and Celtic laziness: through an artistic aversion to coarse scenes and ugly words: through the incapacity to bear resentment of any kind which at that time characterised me: through my dislike of seeing life made bitter and uncomely by what to me, with my eyes really fixed on other things, seemed to be mere trifles too petty for more than a moment's thought or interest: – through these reasons, simple as they may sound, I gave up to you always. As a natural result, your claims, your efforts at domination, your exactions grew more and more unreasonable. Your meanest motive, your lowest appetite, your most common passion, became to you laws by which the lives of others were to be guided always, and to which, if necessary, they were to be without scruple sacrificed. Knowing that by making a scene you could always have your way, it was but natural that you should proceeed, almost unconsciously I have no doubt, to every excess of vulgar violence. At the end you did not know to what goal you were hurrying, or with what aim in view. Having made your own of my genius, my will-power, and my fortune, you required, in the blindness of an inexhaustible greed, my entire existence. You took it. At the one supremely and tragically critical moment of all my life, just before my lamentable step of beginning my absurd action, on the one side there was your father attacking me with hideous cards

left at my club, on the other side there was you attacking me with no less loathsome letters. The letter I received from you on the morning of the day I let you take me down to the Police Court to apply for the ridiculous warrant for your father's arrest was one of the worst you ever wrote, and for the most shameful reason. Between you both I lost my head. My judgement forsook me. Terror took its place. I saw no possible escape, I may say frankly, from either of you. Blindly I staggered as an ox into the shambles. I had made a gigantic psychological error. I had always thought that my giving up to you in small things meant nothing: that when a great moment arrived I could reassert my will-power in its natural superiority. It was not so. At the great moment my will-power completely failed me. In life there is really no small or great thing. All things are of equal value and of equal size. My habit – due to indifference chiefly at first – of giving up to you in everything had become insensibly a real part of my nature. Without my knowing it, it had stereotyped my temperament to one permanent and fatal mood. That is why, in the subtle epilogue to the first edition of his essays, Pater says that 'Failure is to form habits.' When he said it the dull Oxford people thought the phrase a mere wilful inversion of the somewhat wearisome text of Aristotelian Ethics, but there is a wonderful, a terible truth hidden in it. I had allowed you to sap my strength of character, and to me the formation of a habit had proved to be not Failure merely but Ruin. Ethically

you had been even still more destructive to me than you had been artistically.

The warrant once granted, your will of course directed everything. At a time when I should have been in London taking wise counsel, and calmly considering the hideous trap in which I had allowed myself to be caught – the booby-trap as your father calls it to the present day – you insisted on my taking you to Monte Carlo, of all revolting places on God's earth, that all day, and all night as well, you might gamble as long as the Casino remained open. As for me – baccarat having no charms for me – I was left alone outside to myself. You refused to discuss even for five minutes the position to which you and your father had brought me. My business was merely to pay your Hotel expenses and your losses. The slightest allusion to the ordeal awaiting me was regarded as a bore. A new brand of champagne that was recommended to us had more interest for you…. On our return to London those of my friends who really desired my welfare implored me to retire abroad, and not to face an impossible trial. You imputed mean motives to them for giving sound advice, and cowardice to me for listening to it. You forced me to stay to brazen it out, if possible, in the box by absurd and silly perjuries. At the end, I was of course arrested and your Father became the hero of the hour: more indeed than the hero of the hour merely: your family now ranks, strangely enough, with the

Immortals: for with the grotesqueness of effect that is as it were a Gothic element in history, and makes Clio the least serious of all the muses, your father will always live among the kind pure-minded parents of Sunday-school literature, your place is with the Infant Samuel, and in the lowest mire of Malebolge I sit between Gilles de Retz and the Marquis de Sade.

Of course I should have got rid of you. I should have shaken you out of my life as a man shakes from his raiment a thing that has stung him. In the most wonderful of all his plays Aeschylus tells us of the great Lord who brings up in his house the lion-cub, the λέοντος ινιν, and loves it because it comes bright-eyed to his call and fawns on him for its food: φαιδρωπος ποτι χειρα, σαίνων τε γαστρος αναγκαις. And the thing grows up and shows the nature of its race ηθος το πρόσθε τοκήων, and destroys the lord and his house and all that he possesses. I feel that I was such a one as he. But my fault was, not that I did not part from you, but that I parted from you far too often. As far as I can make out I ended my friendship with you every three months regularly, and each time that I did so you managed by means of entreating, telegrams, letters, the interposition of your friends, the interposition of mine, and the like to induce me to allow you back. When at the end of March '93 you left my house at Torquay I had determined never to speak to you again, or to allow you under any

circumstances to be with me, so revolting had been the scene you had made the night before your departure. You wrote and telegraphed from Bristol to beg me to forgive you and meet you. Your tutor, who had stayed behind, told me that he thought that at times you were quite irresponsible for what you said and did, and that most, if not all of the men at Magdalen were of the same opinion. I consented to meet you, and of course I forgave you. On the way up to town you begged me to take you to the Savoy. That was indeed a visit fatal to me. Three months later, in June, we are at Goring. Some of your Oxford friends came to stay from a Saturday to Monday. The morning of the day they went away you made a scene so dreadful, so distressing that I told you that we must part. I remember quite well, as we stood on the level croquet-ground with the pretty lawn all round us, pointing out to you that we were spoiling each other's lives, that you were absolutely ruining mine and that I evidently was not making you really happy, and that an irrevocable parting, a complete separation was the one wise philosophic thing to do. You went sullenly after luncheon, leaving one of your most offensive letters behind with the butler to be handed to me after your departure. Before three days had elapsed you were telegraphing from London to beg to be forgiven and allowed to return. I had taken the place to please you. I had engaged you own servants at your request. I was always terribly sorry for the hideous temper

to which you were really a prey. I was fond of you so I let you come back and forgave you. Three months later still, in September new scenes occurred, the occasion of them being my pointing out the schoolboy faults of your attempted translation of *Salomé*. You must by this time be a fair enough French scholar to know that the translation was as unworthy of you, as an ordinary Oxonian, as it was of the work it sought to render. You did not of course know it them, and in one of the violent letters you wrote to me on the point you saw that you were under '*no intellectual obligation of any kind*' to me. I remember that when I read the statement, I felt that it was the one really true thing you had written to me in the whole course of our friendship. I saw that a less cultivated nature would really have suited your mind better. I am not saying this in bitterness at all, but simply as a fact of companionship. Ultimately the bond of all companionship, whether in marriage or in friendship, is conversation, and conversation must have a common basis, and between two people of widely different culture the only common basis possible is the lowest level. The trivial in thought and action is charming. I had made it the keystone of a very brilliant philosophy expressed in plays and paradoxes. But the froth and folly of our life grew often very wearisome to me. It was only in the mire that we met: and fascinating, terribly fascinating though the one topic round which your talk invariably centred was, still at the end it became quite monot-

onous to me: I was often bored to death by it, and accepted it as I accepted your passion for going to music-halls, or your mania for absurd extravagances in eating and drinking, or any other of your to me less attractive characteristics, as a thing, that it is to say, that one simply has to put up with, a part of the high price one paid for knowing you. When after leaving Goring I went to Dinard for a fortnight you were extremely angry with me for not taking you with me, and, before my departure there, made some very unpleasant scenes on the subject at the Albemarle Hotel, and sent me some equally unpleasant telegrams to a county house I was staying at for a few days. I told you, I remember, that I thought it was your duty to be with your own people for a little, as you had passed the whole season away from them. But in reality, to be perfectly frank with you, I could not under any circumstances have let you be with me. We had been together for nearly twelve weeks. I required rest and freedom from the terrible strain of your companionship. It was necessary for me to be a little by myself. It was intellectually necessary. And so I confess I saw in your letter, from which I have quoted, a very good opportunity for ending the fatal friendship that had sprung up between us, and ending it without bitterness, as I had indeed tried to do on that bright June morning at Goring, three months before. It was however represented to me, – I am bound to say candidly by one of my own friends to whom you had

gone in your difficulty – that you would be much hurt, perhaps almost humiliated at having your work sent back to you like a schoolboy's exercise; that I was expecting far too much intellectually from you; and that, no matter what you wrote or did, you were absolutely and entirely devoted to me. I did not want to be the first to check or discourage you in your beginnings in literature: I knew quite well that no translation, unless one done by a poet, could render the colour and cadence of my work in any adequate measure: devotion seemed to me, seems to me still, a wonderful thing, not to be lightly thrown away: so I took the translation and you back. Exactly three months later, after a series of scenes culminating in one more than usually revolting, when you came one Monday evening to my rooms accompanied by two of your friends, I found myself actually flying abroad next morning to escape from you, giving my family some absurd reason for my sudden departure, and leaving a false address with my servant for fear you might follow me by the next train. And I remember that afternoon, as I was in the railway-carriage whirling up to Paris, thinking what an impossible, terrible, utterly wrong state my life had got into, when I, a man of worldwide reputation, was actually forced to run away from England, in order to try and get rid of a friendship that was entirely destructive of everything fine in me either from the intellectual or ethical point of view: the person from whom I was flying being no terrible creature

sprung from sewer or mire into modern life with whom I had entangled my days, but you yourself, a young man of my own social rank and position, who had been at my own college at Oxford, and was an incessant guest at my house. The usual telegrams of entreaty and remorse followed: I disregarded them. Finally you threatened that unless I consented to meet you, you would under no circumstances consent to proceed to Egypt. I had myself, with your knowledge and concurrence, begged your mother to send you to Egypt away from England, as you were wrecking your life in London. I knew that if you did not go it would be a terrible disappointment to her, and for her sake I did meet you, and under the influence of great emotion, which even you cannot have forgotten, I forgave the past; though I said nothing at all about the future. On my return to London next day I remember sitting in my room and sadly and seriously trying to make up my mind whether or not you really were what you seemed to me to be, so full of terrible defects, so utterly ruinous both to yourself and to others, so fatal a one to know even or to be with. For a whole week I thought about it, and wondered if after all I was not unjust and mistaken in my estimate of you. At the end of the week a letter from your mother is handed in. It expressed to the full every feeling I myself had about you. In it she spoke of your blind exaggerated vanity which made you despise your home, and treat your elder brother – that *candiddissima anima*

– 'as a Philistine': of your temper which made her afraid to speak to you about your life, the life she felt, she knew, you were leading: about your conduct in money matters, so distressing to her in more ways than one; of the degeneration and change that had taken place in you. She saw, of course, that heredity had burdened you with a terrible legacy, and frankly admitted it, admitted it with terror: he is 'the one of my children who has inherited the fatal Douglas temperament,' she wrote of you. At the end she stated that she felt bound to declare that your friendship with me, in her opinion, had so intensified your vanity that it had become the source of all your faults, and earnestly begged me not to meet you abroad. I wrote to her at once, in reply, and told her that I agreed entirely with every word she had said. I added much more. I went as far as I could possibly go. I told her that the origin of our friendship was you in your undergraduate days at Oxford coming to beg me to help you in very serious trouble of a very particular character. I told her that your life had been continually in the same manner troubled. The reason of your going to Belgium you had placed to the fault of your companion in that journey, and your mother had reproached me with having introduced you to him. I replaced the fault on the right shoulders, on yours. I assured her at the end that I had not the smallest intention of meeting you abroad, and begged her to try to keep you there, either as an honorary '*attaché*,' if that were

possible, or to learn modern languages, if it were not, or for any reason she chose, at least during two or three years, and for your sake as well as for mine. In the meantime you are writing to me by every post from Egypt. I took not the smallest notice of any of your communications. I read them, and tore them up. I had quite settled to have no more to do with you. My mind was made up, and I gladly devoted myself to the art whose progress I had allowed you to interrupt. At the end of three months, your mother, with that unfortunate weakness of will that characterises her, and that in the tragedy of my life has been an element no less fatal than your father's violence, actually writes to me herself – I have no doubt, of course, at your instigation – tells me that you are extremely anxious to hear from me, and in order that I should have no excuse for not communicating with you, sends me your address in Athens, which, of course, I knew perfectly well. I confess I was absolutely astounded at her letter. I could not understand how, after what she had written to me in December, and what I in answer had written to her, she could in any way try to repair or to renew my unfortunate friendship with you. I acknowledged her letter, of course, and again urged her to try and get you connected with some Embassy abroad, so as to prevent your returning to England, but I did not write to you, or take any more notice of your telegrams than I did before your mother had written to me. Finally you actually telegraphed to my wife

begging her to use her influence with me to get me to write to you. Our friendship had always been a source of distress to her: not merely because she had never liked you person-ally, but because she saw how your continual companionship altered me and not for the better: still, just as she had always been most gracious and hospitable to you, so she could not bear the idea of my being in any way unkind – for so it seemed to her – to any of my friends. She thought, knew indeed, that it was a thing alien to my character. At her request I did communicate with you. I remember the wording of my telegram quite well. I said that time healed every wound but that for many months to come I would neither write to you nor see you. You started without delay for Paris, sending me passionate telegrams on the road to beg me to see you once, at any rate. I declined. You arrived in Paris late on a Saturday night, and found a brief letter from me waiting for you at your Hotel stating that I would not see you. Next morning I receive in Tite St. a telegram of some ten or eleven pages in length from you. You stated in it that no matter what you had done to me you could not believe that I would absolutely decline to see you: you reminded me that for the sake of seeing me even for one hour you had travelled six days and nights across Europe without stopping once on the way: you made what I must admit was a most pathetic appeal, and ended with what seemed to me a threat of suicide, and one not thinly veiled. You had yourself

often told me how many of your race there had been who had stained their hands in their own blood; your uncle certainly, your grandfather possibly; many others in the mad, bad line from which you come. Pity, my old affection for you, regard for your mother to whom your death under such dreadful circumstances would have been a blow almost too great for her to bear, the horror of the idea that so young a life, and one that amidst all its ugly faults had still promise of beauty in it, should come so revolting an end, mere humanity itself – all these, if excuses be necessary, must serve as my excuse for consenting to accord you one last interview. When I arrived in Paris, your tears, breaking out again and again all through the evening, and falling over your cheeks like rain as we sat, at dinner first at Voisin's, at supper at Paillard's afterwards: the unfeigned joy you evinced at seeing me, holding my hand whenever you could, as though you were a gentle and penitent child: your contrition, so simple and sincere, at the moment: made me consent to renew our friendship. Two days after we had returned to London, your father saw you having luncheon with me at the Café Royal, joined my table, drank of my wine, and that afternoon, through a letter addressed to you, began his first attack on me... It may be strange, but I had once again, I will not say the chance, but the duty of separating from you forced on me. I need hardly remind you that I refer to your conduct to me at Brighton from October 10th to 13th, 1894. Three

years ago is a long time for you to go back. But we who live in prison, and in whose lives there is no event but sorrow, have to measure time by throbs of pain, and the record of bitter moments. We have nothing else to think of. Suffering – curious as it may sound to you – is the means by which we exist, because it is the only means by which we become conscious of existing; and the remembrance of suffering in the past is necessary to us as the warrant, the evidence of our continued identity. Between myself and the memory of joy lies a gulf no less deep than that between myself and joy in its actuality. Had our life together been as the world fancied it to be, one simply of pleasure, profligacy and laughter, I would not be able to recall a single passage in it. It is because it was full of moments and days tragic, bitter, sinister in their warnings, dull or dreadful in their monotonous scenes and unseemly violences, that I can see or hear each separate incident in its detail, can indeed see or hear little else. So much in this place do men live by pain that my friendship with you, in the way through which I am forced to remember it, appears to me always as a prelude consonant with those varying modes of anguish which each day I have to realise; nay more to necessitate them even; as though my life, whatever it had seemed to myself and to others, had all the while been a real Symphony of Sorrow, passing through its rhythmically-linked movements to its certain resolution, with the inevitableness that in art char-

acterises the treatment of every great theme... I spoke of your conduct to me on three successive days, three years ago, did I not? I was trying to finish my last play at Worthing by myself. The two visits you had paid to me had ended. You suddenly appeared a third time bringing with you a companion whom you actually proposed should stay in my house. I, (you must admit now quite properly,) absolutely declined. I entertained you, of course; I had no option in the matter: but elsewhere: and not in my own home. The next day, a Monday, your companion returned to the duties of his profession, and you stayed with me. Bored with Worthing, and still more, I have no doubt, with my fruitless efforts to concentrate my attention on my play, the only thing that really interested me at the moment, you insist on being taken to the Grand Hotel, at Brighton. The night we arrive you fall ill with that dreadful low fever that is foolishly called the influenza, your second, if not third attack. I need not remind you how I waited on you, and tended you, not merely with every luxury of fruit, flowers, presents, books, and the like that money can procure, but with that affection, tenderness and love that, whatever you may think, is not to be procured for money. Except for an hour's walk in the morning, an hour's drive in the afternoon I never left the Hotel. I got special grapes from London for you, as you did not care for those the Hotel supplied, invented things to please you, remained either with you or in the room next

to yours, sat with you every evening to quiet or amuse you. After four or five days you recover, and I take lodgings in order to try and finish my play. You, of course, accompany me. The morning after the day on which we were installed I feel extremely ill. You have to go to London on business, but promise to return in the afternoon. In London you meet a friend, and do not come back to Brighton till late the next day by which time I am in a terrible fever, and the Doctor finds I have caught the influenza from you. Nothing could have been more uncomfortable for anyone ill than the lodgings turn out to be. My sitting room is on the first floor, my bedroom on the third. There is no manservant to wait on me, not even anyone to send out on a message, or to get what the Doctor orders. But you are there. I feel no alarm. The next two days you leave me entirely alone without care, without attendance, without anything. It was not a question of grapes, flowers, and charming gifts: it was a question of mere necessaries: I could not even get the milk the Doctor had ordered for me; lemonade was pronounced an impossibility: and when I begged you to procure me a book at the booksellers, or if they had not got whatever I had fixed on to choose something else, you never even take the trouble to go there. And when I was left all day without anything to read in consequence, you calmly tell me that you bought me the book and that they promised to send it down, a statement which I found out by chance afterwards to have

been entirely untrue from beginning to end. All the while you are of course living at my expense, driving about, dining at the Grand Hotel, and indeed only appearing in my room for money. On the Saturday night, you having left me completely unattended and alone since the morning, I asked you to come back after dinner, and sit with me for a little. With irritable voice and ungracious manner you promise to do so. I wait till eleven oc. and you never appear. I then left a note for you in your room just reminding you of the promise you had made me, and how you had kept it. At three in the morning, unable to sleep, and tortured with thirst, I made my way, in the dark and cold, down to the sitting room in the hopes of finding some water there. I found *you*. You fell on me with every hideous word an intemperate mood, an undisciplined and untutored nature could suggest. By the terrible alchemy of egotism you converted your remorse into rage. You accused me of self-ishness in expecting you to be with me when I was ill; of standing between you and your amusements; of trying to deprive you of your pleasures. You told me, and I know it was quite true, that you had come back at midnight simply in order to change your dress-clothes, and go out again to where you hoped new pleasures were waiting for you, but that by leaving for you a letter in which I had reminded you that you had neglected me the whole day and the whole evening, I had really robbed you of your desire for more

enjoyments, and diminished your actual capacity for fresh delights. I went back upstairs in disgust, as and remained sleepless till dawn, nor till long after dawn was I able to get anything to quench the thirst of the fever that was on me. At eleven o'clock you came into my room. In the previous scene I could not help observing that by my letter I had, at any rate, checked you in a night of more than usual excess. In the morning you were quite yourself. I waited naturally to hear what excuses you had to make, and in what way you were going to ask for the forgiveness that you knew in your heart was invariably waiting for you, no matter what you did; your absolute trust that I would always forgive you being the thing in you that I always really liked the best, perhaps the best thing in you to like. So far from doing that, you began to repeat the same scene with renewed emphasis and more violent assertion: I told you at length to leave the room: you pretended to do so, but when I lifted up my head from the pillow in which I had buried it, you were still there, and with brutality of laughter and hysteria of rage you moved suddenly towards me. A sense of horror came over me, for what exact reason I could not make out; but I got out of my bed at once, and bare-footed and just as I was, made my way down the two flights of stairs to the sitting room, which I did not leave till the owner of the lodgings – whom I had rung for – had assured me that you had left my bedroom, and promised to remain within call, in case of

necessity. After an interval of an hour, during which time the Doctor had come and found me, of course, in a state of absolute nervous prostration, as well as in a worse condition of fever than I had been at the outset, you returned silently, for money: took what you could find on the dressing-table and mantelpiece; and left the house with your luggage. Need I tell you what I thought of you during the two wretched lonely days of illness that followed? Is it necessary for me to state, that I saw clearly that it would be a dishonour to myself to continue even an acquaintance with such a one as you had showed yourself to be? That I recognised that the ultimate moment had come, and recognised it as being really a great relief? And that I knew that for the future my Art and Life would be freer and better and more beautiful in every possible way? Ill as I was, I felt at ease. The fact that the separation was irrevocable gave me peace. By Tuesday the fever had left me, and for the first time I dined downstairs. Wednesday was my birthday. Amongst the telegrams and communications on my table was a letter in your handwriting. I opened it with a sense of sadness over me. I knew that the time had gone by when a pretty phrase, an expression of affection, a word of sorrow would make me take you back. But I was entirely deceived. I had underrated you. The letter you sent to me on my birthday was an elaborate repetition of the two scenes, set cunningly and carefully down in black and white! You mocked me with common

jests. Your one satisfaction in the whole affair was, you said, that you retired to the Grand Hotel, and entered your luncheon to my account before you left for Town. You congratulated me on my prudence in leaving my sickbed, on my sudden flight downstairs. '*It was an ugly moment for you*', you said, '*uglier than you imagine.*' Ah! I felt it but too well. What it had really meant I did not know: whether you had with you the pistol you had bought to try and frighten your father with, and that, thinking it to be unloaded, you had once fired off in a public restaurant in my company: whether your hand was moving towards a common dinner-knife that by chance was lying on the table between us; whether forgetting in your rage your low stature and inferior strength you had thought of some specially personal insult, or attack even, as I lay ill there: I could not tell. I do not know to the present moment. All I know is that a feeling of utter horror had come over me, and that I had felt that unless I left the room at once, and got away, you would have done, or tried to do something that would have been, even to you, a source of lifelong shame. Only once before in my life had I experienced such a feeling of horror at any human being. It was when in my library at Tite Street, waving his small hands in the air in epileptic fury, your Father, with his bully, or his friend, between us, had stood uttering every foul word his foul mind could think of, and screaming the loathsome threats he afterwards with such cunning carried

out. In the latter case he, of course, was the one who had to leave the room first. I drove him out. In your case I went. It was not the first time I had been obliged to save you from yourself.... You concluded your letter by saying, '*When you are not on your pedestal you are not interesting. The next time you are ill, I will go away at once.*' Ah! What coarseness of fibre does that reveal! What an entire lack of imagination! How callous, how common had the temperament by that time become!... '*When you are not on your pedestal you are not interesting. The next time you are ill I will go away at once.*' How often have those words come back to me in the wretched solitary cell of the various prisons I have been sent to. I have said them to myself over and over again, and seen in them, I hope unjustly, some of the secret of your strange silence. For you to write thus to me, when the very illness and fever from which I was suffering I had caught from tending you, was of course revolting in its coarseness and crudity; but for any human being in the whole world to write thus to another would be a sin for which there is no pardon, were there any sin for which there is none... I confess that when I had finished your letter I felt almost polluted, as if by associating with one of such a nature I had soiled and shamed my life irretrievably. I had, it is true, done so, but I was not to learn how fully till just six months later on in life. I settled with myself to go back to London on the Friday, and see Sir George Lewis personally and request

him to write to your Father to state that I had determined never under any circumstances to allow you to enter my house, to sit at my board, to talk to me, walk with me, or anywhere and at any time to be my companion at all. This done I would have written to you just to inform you of the course of action I had adopted, the reasons you would inevitably have realised for yourself. I had everything arranged on Thursday night, when on Friday morning, as I was sitting at breakfast before starting, I happened to open the newspaper and saw in it a telegram stating that your elder brother, the real head of the family, the heir to the title, the pillar of the house, had been found dead in a ditch with his gun lying discharged beside him. The horror of the circumstances of the tragedy, now known to have been an accident, but then stained with a darker suggestion; the pathos of the sudden death of one so loved by all who knew him, and almost on the eve, as it were, of his marriage; my idea of what your own sorrow would, or should be; my consciousness of the misery awaiting your mother at the loss of the one to whom she clung for comfort and joy in life, and who, as she told me once herself, had from the very day of his birth never caused her to shed a single tear; my consciousness of your own isolation, both your other brothers being out of Europe, and you consequently the only one to whom your mother and sister could look, not merely for companionship in their sorrow, but also for those dreary responsibilities of

dreadful detail that Death always brings with it; the mere sense of the '*lacrimae rerum*', of the tears of which the world is made, and of the sadness of all human things; … out of the confluence of these thoughts and emotions crowding into my brain came infinite pity for you and your family. My own griefs and bitternesses against you I forgot. What you had been to me in my sickness, I could not be to you in your bereavement. I telegraphed at once to you my deepest sympathy, and in the letter that followed invited you to come to my house as soon as you were able. I felt that to abandon you at that particular moment, and formally through a solicitor, would have been too terrible for you…. On your return to town from the actual scene of the tragedy to which you had been summoned, you came at once to me very sweetly and simply, in your suit of woe, and with your eyes dim with tears. You sought consolation and help, as a child might seek it. I opened to you my house, my home, my heart. I made your sorrow mine also, that you might have help in bearing it. Never, even by one word, did I allude to your conduct towards me, to the revolting scenes, or the revolting letters. Your grief, which was real, seemed to me to bring you nearer to me than you had ever been. The flowers you took from me to put on your brother's grave were to be a symbol not merely of the beauty of his life, but of the beauty that in all lives lies dormant and may be brought to light…. The Gods are strange. It is not of our vices only they make instruments

De Profundis

to scourge us. They bring us to ruin through what in us is good, gentle, humane, loving. But for my pity and affection for you and yours, I would not now be weeping in this terrible place.

Of course I discern in all our relations, not Destiny merely, but Doom: Doom that walks always swiftly, because she goes to the shedding of blood. Through your father you come of a race, marriage with whom is horrible, friendship fatal, and that lays violent hands either on its own life, or on the lives of others. In every little circumstance in which the ways of our lives met; in every point of great, or seemingly trivial import in which you came to me for pleasure or for help; in the small chances, the slight accidents that look, in their relation to life, to be no more than the dust that dances in a beam, on the leaf that flutters from a tree, Ruin followed, like the echo of a bitter cry, or the shadow that hunts with the beast of prey. Our friendship really begins with your begging me in a most pathetic and charming letter to assist you in a position appalling to anyone, doubly so to a young man at Oxford: I do so, and ultimately through you using my name as your friend with Sir George Lewis, I begin to lose his esteem and friendship, a friendship of fifteen years standing. When I was deprived of his advice and help and regard I was deprived of the one great safeguard of my life. You send me a very nice poem, of the undergraduate school of verse, for my approval; I reply by a letter

49

of fantastic literary conceits: I compare you to Hylas, or Hyacinth, Jonquil or Narcisse, or some one whom the great god of Poetry favoured, and honoured with his love. The letter is like a passage from one of Shakespeare's sonnets, transposed to a minor key. It can only be understood by those who have read the Symposium of Plato, or caught the spirit of a certain grave mood made beautiful for us in Greek marbles. It was, – let me say frankly – the sort of letter I would, in a happy if wilful moment, have written to any graceful young man of either university who had sent me a poem of his own making, certain that he would have sufficient wit or culture to interpret rightly its fantastic phrases. Look at the history of that letter! It passes from you into the hands of a loathsome companion: from him to a gang of blackmailers: copies of it are sent about London to my friends, and to the manager of the theatre where my work is being performed: every construction, but the right one, is put on it: society is thrilled with the absurd rumour that I have had to pay a huge sum of money for having written an infamous letter to you: this forms the basis of your Father's worst attack: I produce the original letter myself in Court to show what it really is: it is denounced by your Father's counsel as a revolting and insidious attempt to corrupt Innocence: ultimately it forms part of a criminal charge: the crown takes it up: the Judge sums up on it with little learning and much morality: I go to prison for it at last. That is the

result of writing you a charming letter. While I am staying with you at Salisbury you are terribly alarmed at a threatening communication from a former companion of yours: you beg me to see the writer and help you: I do so: the result is Ruin to me. I am forced to take everything you have done on my own shoulders and answer for it. When, having failed to take your degree, you have to go down from Oxford, you telegraph to me in London to beg me to come to you: I do so at once: you ask me to take you to Goring, as you did not like, under the circumstances, to go home: at Goring you see a house that charms you: I take it for you: the result from every point of view is Ruin to me. One day you come to me and ask me, as a personal favour to you, to write something for an Oxford undergraduate magazine, about to be started by some friend of yours, whom I had never heard of in all my life, and knew nothing at all about. To please you – what did I not do to please you? – I send him a page of paradoxes destined originally for the *Saturday Review*. A few months later I find myself standing in the dock of the Old Bailey on account of the character of the magazine. It forms part of the Crown charge against me. I am called upon to defend your friend's prose and your own verse. The former I cannot palliate; the latter I, loyal, to the bitter extreme, to your youthful literature as to your youthful life, do very strongly defend, and will not hear of your being a writer of indecencies. But I go to prison, all the same, for

your friend's undergraduate magazine and 'The Love that dares not tell its name.' At Christmas I give you a 'very pretty present', as you described it in your letter of thanks, worth some £40 or £50 at most. When the crash of my life comes, and I am ruined, the bailiff who seizes my library, and has it sold, does so to pay for the 'very pretty present.' It was for that, the execution was put into my house. At the ultimate and terrible moment when I am taunted, and spurred-on by your taunts, to take an action against your Father and have him arrested, the last straw to which I clutch in my wretched efforts to escape, is the terrible expense. I tell the Solicitor in your presence that I have no funds, that I cannot possibly afford the appalling cost, that I have no money at my disposal. What I said was, as you know, perfectly true. On that fatal Friday instead of being in Humphrey's office weakly consenting to my own ruin, I would have been free and happy in France, away from you and your Father, unconscious of his loathsome card, and indifferent to your letters, if I had been able to leave the Avondale Hotel. But the Hotel people absolutely refused to allow me to go. You had been staying with me for ten days: indeed you had ultimately, to my great, and you will admit, rightful indignation, brought a companion of yours to stay with me also: my bill for the ten days was nearly £140. The proprietor said he could not allow my luggage to be removed from the Hotel till I had paid the account in full. That is

what kept me in London. Had it not been for the Hotel bill I would have gone to Paris on Thursday morning... When I told the Solicitor I had no money to face the gigantic expense, you interposed at once. You said that your own family would be only too delighted to pay all the necessary costs: that your Father had been an incubus to them all: that they had often discussed the possibility of getting him put into a lunatic asylum so as to keep him out of the way: that he was a daily source of annoyance and distress to your mother and to everyone else; that if I would only come forward to have him shut up I would be regarded by the family as the champion and their benefactor: and that your mother's rich relations themselves would look on it as a real delight to be allowed to pay all costs and expenses that might be incurred in any such effort. The Solicitor closed at once, and I was hurried to the Police Court. I had no excuse left for not going. I was forced into it. Of course your family don't pay the costs, and, when I am made bankrupt, it is by your Father, and *for* the costs – the meagre balance of them – some £700. At the present moment my wife, estranged from me over the important question of whether I should have £3 or £3.10 a week to live on, is preparing a divorce suit, for which, of course, entirely new evidence and an entirely new trial, to be followed perhaps by more serious proceedings, will be necessary. I, naturally, know nothing of the details. I merely know the name of the witness on whose

evidence my wife's solicitors rely. It is your own Oxford servant, whom at your special request I took into my service for our summer at Goring.... But, indeed, I need not go on further with more instances of the strange Doom you seem to have brought on me in all things big or little. It makes me feel sometimes as if you yourself had been merely a puppet worked by some secret and unseen hand to bring terrible events to a terrible issue. But puppets themselves have passions. They will bring a new plot into what they are presenting, and twist the ordered issue of vicissitude to suit some whim or appetite of their own. To be entirely free, and at the same time entirely dominated by law, is the eternal paradox of human life that we realise at every moment; and this, I often think, is the only explanation possible of your nature, if indeed in the profound and terrible mysteries of a human soul there is any explanation at all, except one that makes the mystery more marvellous still.

Of course you had your illusions, lived in them indeed, and through their shifting mists and coloured veils saw all things changed. You thought, I remember quite well, that your devoting yourself to me, to the entire exclusion of your family and family life, was a proof of your wonderful appreciation of me, and your great affection. No doubt to you it seemed so. But recollect that with me was luxury, high living, unlimited pleasure, money without stint. Your family life bored you. The 'cold cheap wine of Salisbury',

to use a phrase of your own making, was distasteful to you. On my side, and along with my intellectual attractions, were the fleshpots of Egypt. When you could not find me to be with, the companions whom you chose as substitutes were not flattering.... You thought again that in sending a lawyer's letter to your Father to say that, rather than sever your eternal friendship with me, you would give up the allowance of £250 a year which, with I believe deductions for your Oxford debts, he was then making you, you were realising the very chivalry of friendship touching the noblest note of self-denial. But your surrender of your little allowance did not mean that you were ready to give up even one of your most superfluous luxuries, or most unnecessary extravagances. On the contrary. Your appetite for luxurious living was never so keen. My expenses for eight days in Paris for myself, you, and your Italian servant were nearly £150: Paillard alone absorbing £85. At the rate at which you wished to live, your entire income for a whole year, if you had taken your meals alone, and been especially economical in your selection of the cheaper form of pleasures, would hardly have lasted you for three weeks. The fact that in what was merely a pretence of bravado you had surrendered your allowance, such as it was, gave you at last a plausible reason for your claim to live at my expense, or what you that a plausible reason: and on many occasions you seriously availed yourself of it, and gave the very fullest

expression to it; and the continued drain, principally of course on me, but also to a certain extent, I know, on your mother, was never so distressing, because in my case, at any rate, never so completely unaccompanied by the smallest word of thanks, or sense of limit.... You thought again that in attacking your own Father with dreadful letters, abusive telegrams, and insulting postcards you were really fighting your mother's battles, coming forward as her champion, and avenging the no doubt terrible wrongs and sufferings of her married life. It was quite an illusion on your part; one of your worst, indeed. The way for you to have avenged your mother's wrongs on your Father, if you considered it part of a son's duty to do so, was by being a better son to your mother than you had been: by not making her afraid to speak to you on serious things: by not signing bills the payment of which devolved on her: by being gentler to her, and not bringing sorrow into her days. Your brother Francis made great amends to her for what she had suffered, by his sweetness and goodness to her through the brief years of his flower-like life. You should have taken him as your model. You were wrong then in fancying that it would have been an absolute delight and joy to your mother if you *had* managed through me to get your father put into prison. I feel sure you were wrong. And if you want to know what a woman really feels when her husband, and the father of her children, is in prison dress, in a prison cell, write to my

De Profundis

wife and ask her. She will tell you... *I* also had my illusions.
I thought life was going to be a brilliant comedy, and that
you were to be one of many graceful figures in it. I found
it to be a revolting and repellent tragedy, and that the sinister
occasion of the great catastrophe, sinister in its concentration
of aim and intensity of narrowed will-power, was yourself,
stripped of that mask of joy and pleasure by which you, no
less than I, had been deceived and led astray.

You can now understand – can you not? – a little of what
I am suffering. Some paper, *The Pall Mall Gazette* I think,
describing the dress-rehearsal of one of my plays, spoke of
you as following me about like my shadow: the memory of
our friendship is the shadow that walks with me here: that
seems never to leave me: that wakes me up at night to tell
me the same story over and over till its wearisome iteration
makes all sleep abandon me till dawn: at dawn it begins
again: it follows me into the prison-yard and makes me talk
to myself as I tramp round: each detail that accompanied
each dreadful moment I am forced to recall: there is nothing
that happened in those ill-starred years that I cannot recreate
in that chamber of the brain which is set apart for grief or
for despair: every strained note of your voice, every twitch
and gesture of your nervous hands, every bitter word, every
poisonous phrase comes back to me: remember the street
or river down which we are passed, the wall or woodland
that surrounded us, at which figure on the dial stood the

hands of the clock, which way went the wings of the wind, the shape and colour of the moon.

There is, I know, one answer to all that I have said to you, and that is that you loved me: that all through those two and a half years during which the Fates were weaving into one scarlet pattern the threads of our divided lives you really loved me. Yes: I know you did. No matter what your conduct to me was I always felt that at heart you really did love me. Though I saw quite clearly that my position in the world of art, the interest my personality had always excited, my money, the luxury in which I lived, the thousand and one things that went to make up a life so charmingly, so wonderfully improbable as mine was, were, each and all of them, elements that fascinated you and made you cling to me: yet besides all this there was something more, some strange attraction for you: you loved me far better than you loved anybody else. But you, like myself, have had a terrible tragedy in your life, though one of an entirely opposite character to mine. Do you want to learn what it was? It was this. In you Hate was always stronger than Love. Your hatred of your Father was of such stature that it entirely outstripped, o'erthrew, and overshadowed your love of me. There was no struggle between them at all, or but little; of such dimensions was your Hatred and of such monstrous growth. You did not realise that there is no room for both passions in the same soul. They cannot live together in that fair carven house. Love is fed by the imag-

ination, by which we become wiser than we know, better than we feel, nobler than we are: by which we can see Life as a whole; by which, and by which alone, we can understand others in their real as in their ideal relations. Only what is fine, and finely conceived, can feed Love. But anything will feed Hate. There was not a glass of champagne you drank, not a rich dish you ate of in all those years that did not feed your Hate and make it fat. So to gratify it, you gambled with my life, as you gambled with my money, carelessly, recklessly, indifferent to the consequence. If you lost, the loss would not, you fancied, be yours. If you won, yours, you knew, would be the exultation, and the advantages of victory.

Hate blinds people. You were not aware of that. Love can read the writing on the remotest star, but Hate so blinded you that you could see no further than the narrow, walled-in, and already lust-withered garden of your common desires. Your terrible lack of imagination, the one really fatal defect of your character, was entirely the result of the Hate that lived in you. Subtly, silently and in secret, Hate gnawed at your nature, as the lichen bites at the root of some sallow plant, till you grew to see nothing but the most meagre interests and the most petty aims. That faculty in you which Love would have fostered, Hate poisoned and paralysed. When your father first began to attack me, it was as your private friend, and in a private letter to you. As soon as I had read the letter, with its obscene threats and coarse

violences, I saw at once that a terrible danger was looming on the horizon of my troubled days: I told you I would not be the catspaw between you both in your ancient hatred of each other: that I in London was naturally much bigger game for him than a Secretary for Foreign Affairs at Homburg: that it would be unfair to me to place me even for a moment in such a position: and that I had something better to do with my life than to have scenes with a man drunken, declassé and half-witted as he was. You could not be made to see this. Hate blinded you. You insisted that the quarrel had really nothing to do with me: that you would not allow your Father to dictate to you in your private friendships: that it would be most unfair of me to interfere. You had already, before you saw me on the subject, sent your Father a foolish and vulgar telegram, as your answer. That of course committed you to a foolish and vulgar course of action to follow. The fatal errors of life are not due to man's being unreasonable: an unreasonable moment may be one's finest moment. They are due to man's being logical. There is a wide difference. That telegram conditioned the whole of your subsequent relations with your Father, and consequently the whole of my life. And the grotesque thing about it is that it was a telegram of which the commonest streetboy would have been ashamed. From pert telegrams to priggish lawyers' letters was a natural progress, and the result of your lawyer's letters to your Father was, of course,

to urge him on still further. You left him no option but to go on. You forced it on him as a point of honour, or of dishonour rather, that your appeal should have the more effect. So the next time he attacks me, no longer in a private letter and as your private friend, but in public and as a public man. I have to expel him from my house. He goes from Restaurant to Restaurant looking for me, in order to insult me before the whole world, and in such a manner that if I retaliated I would be ruined, and if I did not retaliated I would be ruined also. *Then* surely was the time when *you* should have come forward, and said that you would not expose me to such hideous attacks, such infamous persecution, on your account, but would, readily and at once, resign any claim you had to my friendship? You feel that now, I suppose. But it never even occurred to you then. Hate blinded you. All you could think of, (besides of course writing to him insulting letters and telegrams,) was to buy a ridiculous pistol that goes off in The Berkeley, under circumstances that create a worse scandal than ever came to *your* ears. Indeed the idea of your being the object of a terrible quarrel between your Father and a man of my position seemed to delight you. It, I suppose very naturally, pleased your vanity, and flattered your self-importance. That your father might have had your body, which did not interest me, and left me your soul, which did not interest him, would have been to you a distressing solution of the question. You scented the chance of a public

scandal and flew to it. The prospect of a battle in which you would be safe delighted you. I never remember you in higher spirits than you were for the rest of that season. Your only disappointment seemed to be that nothing actually happened, and that no further meeting or fracas had taken place between us. You consoled yourself by sending him telegrams of such a character that at last the wretched man wrote to you and said that he had given orders to his servants, that no telegram was to be brought to him under any pretence whatsoever. That did not daunt you. You saw the immense opportunities afforded by the open postcard, and availed yourself of them to the full. You hounded him on in the chase still more. I do not suppose he would ever really have given it up. Family instincts were strong in him. His hatred of you was just as persistent as your hatred of him, and I was the stalking horse for both [of] you, and a mode of attack as well as a mode of shelter. His very passion for notoriety was not merely individual, but racial. Still, if his interest had flagged for a moment your letters and postcards would soon have quickened it to its ancient flame. They did so. And he naturally went further still. Having assailed me as a private gentleman and in private, as a public man and in public, he ultimately determines to make his final and great attack on me as an artist and in the place where my Art is being represented. He secures by fraud a seat for the first night of one of my plays, and continues to plot to interrupt the

performance, to make a foul speech about me to the audience, to insult my actors, or throw offensive and indecent missiles at me when I am called before the curtain at the close, utterly in some hideous way to ruin me through my work. By the merest chance, in the brief and accidental sincerity of a more than usually intoxicated mood, he boasts of his intention before others. Information is given to the police, and he is kept out of the theatre. You had your chance then. Then was your opportunity. Don't you realise now that you should have seen it, and come forward and said that you would not have my Art, at any rate, ruined for your sake? You knew what my Art was to me, the great primal note by which I had revealed, first myself to myself, and then myself to the world; the real passion of my life; the love to which all other loves were as marsh-water to red wine, or the glow-worm of the marsh to the magic mirror of the moon. Don't you understand now that your lack of imagination was the one really fatal defect of your character? What you had to do was quite simple, and quite clear before you, but Hate had blinded you, and you could see nothing. I could not apologise to your Father for his having insulted me and persecuted me in the most loathsome manner for nearly nine months. I could not get rid of you out of my life. I had tried it again and again. I had gone so far as actually leaving England and going abroad in the hope of escaping from you. It had all been of no use. You were the only person

who could have done anything. The key of the situation rested entirely with yourself. It was the one great opportunity you had of making some slight return to me for all the love and affection and kindness and generosity and care I had shown you. Had you appreciated me even at a tenth of my value as an artist you would have done so. But Hate blinded you. The faculty 'by which, and by which alone, one can understand others in their real, as in their ideal relations': was dead in you. You thought simply of how to get your father into prison. To see him 'in the dock', as you used to say; that was your one idea. The phrase became one of the many *scies* of your daily conversation. One heard it at every meal. Well, you had your desire gratified. Hate granted you every single thing you wished for. It was an indulgent Master to you. It is so, indeed, to all who serve it. For two days you sat on a high seat with the Sheriffs, and feasted your eyes with the spectacle of your Father standing in the dock of the Central Criminal Court. And on the third day I took his place. What had occurred? In your hideous game of hate together, you had both thrown dice for my soul, and you happened to have lost. That was all.

You see that I have to write your life to you, and you have to realise it. We have known each other now for more than four years. Half of the time we have been together: the other half I have had to spend in prison as the result of our friendship. Where you will receive this letter, if indeed it

ever reaches you, I don't know. Rome, Naples, Paris, Venice, some beautiful city on sea or river, I have no doubt, holds you. You are surrounded, if not with all the useless luxury you had with me, at any rate with everything that is pleasurable to eye, ear, and taste. Life is quite lovely to you. And yet, if you are wise, and wish to find Life much lovelier still, and in a different manner, you will let the reading of this terrible letter – for such I know it is – prove to you as important a crisis and turning point of your life as the writing of it is to me. Your pale face used to flush easily with wine or pleasure. If, as you read what is here written, it from time to time becomes scorched, as though by a furnace-vent, with shame, it will be all the better for you. The supreme vice is shallowness. Whatever is realised is right.

I have now got as far as the House of Detention, have I not? After a night passed in the Police Cells I am sent there in the van. You were most attentive and kind. Almost every afternoon, if not actually every afternoon till you go abroad, you took the trouble to drive up to Holloway to see me. You also wrote very sweet and nice letters. But that it was not your Father but you who had put me into prison, that from beginning to end you were the responsible person, that it was through you, for you, and by you that I was there, never for one instant dawned upon you. Even the spectacle of me behind the bars of a wooden cage could not quicken that dead unimaginative nature. You had the sympathy and

the sentimentality of the spectators of a rather pathetic play. That you were the true author of the hideous tragedy did not occur to you. I saw that you realised nothing of what you had done. I did not desire to be the one to tell you what your own heart should have told you, what it indeed would have told you, if you had not let Hate harden it and make it insensate. Everything must come to one out of one's own nature. There is no use in telling a person a thing that they don't feel and can't understand. If I write to you now as I do it is because your own silence and conduct during my long imprisonment have made it necessary. Besides, as things had turned out, the blow had fallen upon me alone. That was a source of pleasure to me. I was content for many reasons to suffer, though there was always to my eyes, as I watched you, something not a little contemptible in your complete and wilful blindness. I remember your producing with absolute pride a letter you had published in one of the halfpenny newspapers bout me. It was a very prudent, temperate, indeed commonplace production. You appealed to the '*English sense of fair play*', or something very dreary of that kind, on behalf of '*a man who was down.*' It was the sort of letter you might have written had a painful change been brought against some respectable person with whom personally you had been quite unacquainted. But you thought it a wonderful letter. You looked on it as a proof of almost Quixotic chivalry. I am aware that you wrote other letters

to other newspapers that they did not publish. But then they were simply to say that you hated your Father. Nobody cared if you did or not. Hate, you have yet to learn, is, intellectually considered, the Eternal negation. Considered from the point of view of the emotions it is a form of Atrophy, and kills everything but itself. To write to the papers to say that one hates someone else is as if one were to write to the papers to say that one has some secret and shameful malady. The fact that the man you hated was your own father, and that the feeling was thoroughly reciprocated, did not make your Hate noble or fine in any way. If it showed anything, it was simply that it was an hereditary disease.... I remember again, when an execution was put into my house, and my books and furniture were seized and advertised to be sold, and Bankruptcy was impending, I naturally wrote to tell you about it. I did not mention that it was to pay for some gifts of mine to you that the bailiffs had entered the home where you had so often dined. I thought, rightly or wrongly, that such news might pain you a little. I merely told you the bare facts. I thought it proper that you should know them. You wrote back from Boulogne in a strain of almost lyrical exultation. You said that you knew your Father was 'hard up for money', and had been obliged to raise £1500 for the expenses of the trial, and that my going Bankrupt was really a 'splendid score' off him, as he would not then be able to get any of his costs out of me! Do you realise now what

Hate blinding a person is? Do you recognise now that when I described it as an Atrophy, destructive of every thing but itself, I was scientifically describing a real psychological fact? That all my charming things were to be sold: my Burne-Jones drawings; my Whistler drawings; my Monticelli; my Simeon Solomons; my china; my Library with its collection of presentation volumes from almost every post of my time, from Hugo to Whitman, from Swinburne to Mallarmé, from Morris to Verlaine; with 15 beautifully bound editions of my father's and mother's works; its wonderful array of College and school prizes; its *editions de luxe*, and the like; was absolutely nothing to you. You said it was a great bore: that was all. What you really saw in it was the possibility that your Father might ultimately lose a few hundred pounds, and that paltry consideration filled you with ecstatic joy. As for the costs of the trial, you may be interested to know that your Father openly said in the Orleans Club that if it had cost him £20,000 he would have considered the money thoroughly well spent, he had extracted such enjoyment, and delight, and triumph out of it all. The fact that he was not able merely to put me into prison for two years, but to take me out for an afternoon and make me a public bankrupt was an extra-refinement of pleasure that he had not expected. It was the crowning-point of my humiliation, and of his complete and perfect victory. Had your Father had no claim for his costs on me, you, I know perfectly well, would as far

as words go, at any rate have been most sympathetic about the entire loss of my library, a loss irreparable to a man of letters, the one of all my material losses the most distressing to me. You might even, remembering the sums of money I had lavishly spent on you and how you had lived on me for years, have taken the trouble to buy in some of my books for me. The best all went in less than £150: about as much as I would spend on you in an ordinary week. But the mean small pleasure of thinking that your Father was going to be a few pence out of pocket made you forget all about trying to make me a little return, so slight, so easy, so inexpensive, so obvious, and so enormously welcome to me, had you brought it about. Am I right in saying that Hate blinds people? Do you see it now? If you don't, try to see it.

How clearly I saw it then, as now, I need not tell you. But I said to myself *'At all costs I must keep Love in my heart. If I go into prison without Love what will become of my soul?'* The letters I wrote to you at that time from Holloway were my efforts to keep Love as the dominant note of my own nature. I could if I had chosen have torn you to pieces with bitter reproaches. I could have rent you with maledictions. I could have held up a mirror to you, and shown you such an image of yourself that you would not have recognised it as your own till you found it mimicking back your gestures of horror, and then you would have known whose shape it was, and hated it and yourself for ever, more than that indeed.

The sins of another were being placed to my account. Had I so chosen, I could on either trial have saved myself at his expense, not from shame indeed but from imprisonment. Had I cared to show that the Crown witnesses – the three most important – had been carefully coached by your Father and his Solicitors, not in reticences merely, but in assertions, in the absolute transference, deliberate, plotted, and rehearsed, of the actions and doings of someone else on to me, I could have had each one of them dismissed from the box by the Judge, more summarily than even wretched perjured Atkins was. I could have walked out of Court with my tongue in my cheek, and my hands in my pockets, a free man. The strongest pressure was put upon me to do so. I was earnestly advised, begged, entreated to do so by people whose sole interest was my welfare, and the welfare of my house. But I refused. I did not choose to do so. I have never regretted my decision for a single moment, even in the most bitter periods of my imprisonment. Such a course of action would have been beneath me. Sins of the flesh are nothing. They are maladies for physicians to cure, if they should be cured. Sins of the soul alone are shameful. To have secured my acquittal by such means would have been a life-long torture to me. But do you really think that you were worthy of the love I was showing you then, or that for a single moment I thought you were? Do you really think that at any period in our friendship you were worthy of the love I showed you,

or that for a single moment I thought you were? I knew you were not. But Love does not traffic in a marketplace, nor use a huckster's scales. Its joy, like the joy of the intellect, is to feel itself alive. The aim of Love is to love: no more, and no less. You were my enemy: such an enemy as no man ever had. I had given you my life, and to gratify the lowest and most contemptible of all human passions, Hatred and Vanity and Greed, you had thrown it away. In less than three years you had entirely ruined me from every point of view. For my own sake there was nothing for me to do but to love you. I knew that if I allowed myself to hate you that in the dry desert of existence over which I had to travel, and am travelling still, every rock would lose its shadow, every palm tree be withered, every well of water prove poisoned at its source. Are you beginning now to understand a little? Is your imagination wakening from the long lethargy in which it has lain? You know already what Hate is. Is it beginning to dawn on you what Love is, and what is the nature of Love? It is not too late for you to learn, though to teach it to you, I may have had to go to a convict's cell?

After my terrible sentence, when the prison-dress was on me, and the prison-house closed, I sat amidst the ruins of my wonderful life, crushed by anguish, bewildered with terror, dazed through pain. But I would not hate you. Every day I said to myself, '*I must keep Love in my heart today, else*

how shall I live through the day.' I reminded myself that you meant no evil, to me at any rate: I set myself to think that you had but drawn a bow at a venture, and that the arrow had pierced a King between the joints of the harness. To have weighed you against the smallest of my sorrows, the meanest of my losses, would have been, I felt, unfair. I determined I would regard you as one suffering too. I forced myself to believe that at last the scales had fallen from your long-blinded eyes. I used to fancy, and with pain, what your horror must have been when you contemplated your terrible handiwork. There were times, even in those dark days, the darkest of all my life, when I actually longed to console you. So sure was I that at last you had realised what you had done. It did not occur to me then that you could have the supreme vice, shallowness. Indeed, it was a real grief to me when I had to let you know that. I was obliged to reserve for family business my first opportunity of receiving a letter: but my brother-in-law had written to me to say that if I would only write once to my wife she would, for my own sake and for our children's sake, take no action for divorce. I felt my duty was to do so. Setting aside other reasons, I could not bear the idea of being separated from Cyril, that beautiful loving, loveable child of mine, my friend of all friends, my companion beyond all companions, one single hair of whose little golden head should have been dearer and of more value to me than, I will not merely say you

from top to toe, but the entire chrysolite of the whole world: was so indeed to me always, though I failed to understand it till too late.... Two weeks after your application, I get news of you. Robert Sherard, the bravest and most chivalrous of all brilliant beings, comes to see me, and amongst other things tells me that in that ridiculous *Mercure de France*, with its absurd affectation of being the true centre of literary corruption, you are about to publish an article on me with specimens of my letters. He asks me if it really was by my wish. I was greatly taken aback, and much annoyed, and gave orders that the thing was to be stopped at once. You had left my letters lying about for blackmailing companions to steal, for Hotel servants to pilfer, for housemaids to sell. That was simply your careless want of appreciation of what I had written to you. But that you should seriously propose to publish selections from the balance was almost incredible to me. And which of my letters were they? I could get no information. That was my first news of you. It displeased me.

The second piece of news followed shortly afterwards. Your Father's solicitors had appeared in the prison, and served me personally with a Bankruptcy notice, for a paltry £700, the amount of their taxed costs. I was adjudged a public insolvent, and ordered to be produced in Court. I felt most strongly, and feel still, and will revert to the subject again, that these costs should have been paid by your family. You had taken personally on yourself the responsibility of stating

that your family would do so. It was that which had made the Solicitor take up the case in the way he did. You were absolutely responsible. Even irrespective of your engagement on your family's behalf you should have felt that as you had brought the whole ruin on me, the least that could have been done was to spare me the additional ignominy of bankruptcy for an absolutely contemptible sum of money, less than half of what I spent on you in three brief summer months at Goring. Of that, however, no more here. I did through the Solicitor's clerk, I fully admit, receive a message from you on the subject, or at any rate in connection with the occasion. The day he came to receive my depositions as statements, he leant across the table – the prison warder being present – and having consulted a piece of paper which he pulled from his pocket, said to me in a low voice, 'Prince Fleur-de-Lys wishes to be remembered to you.' I stared at him. He repeated the message again. I did not know what he meant. 'The gentleman is abroad at present', he added mysteriously. It all flashed across me, and I remember that, for the first and last time in my entire prison life, I laughed. In that laugh was all the scorn of all the world. Prince Fleur-de-Lys! I saw – and subsequent events showed me that I rightly saw – that nothing that had happened had made you realise a single thing. You were in your own eyes still the graceful Prince of a trivial comedy, not the sombre figure of a tragic show. All that had occurred was but as a feather for the cap

that gilds a narrow head, a flower to pink the doublet that hides a heart that Hate, and Hate alone, can warm, that Love, and Love alone, finds cold. Prince Fleur-de-Lys! You were, no doubt, quite right to communicate with me under an assumed name. I myself, at that time, had no name at all. In the great prison where I was then incarcerated, I was merely the figure and letter of a little cell in a long gallery, one of a thousand lifeless numbers, as of a thousand lifeless lives. But surely there were many real names in real history which would have suited you much better, and by which I would have had no difficulty at all in recognising you at once? I did not look for you behind the spangles of a tinsel vizard, one suitable for an amusing masquerade. Ah! Had your soul been, as for its own perfection even it should have been, wounded with sorrow, bowed with remorse, and humble with grief, such was not the disguise it would have chosen beneath whose shadow to seek entrance to the House of Pain! The great things of life are what they seem to be, and for that reason, strange as it may sound to you, are often difficult to interpret. But the little things of life are symbols. We receive our bitter lessons most easily through them. Your seemingly casual choice of a feigned name was, and will remain symbolic. It revealed you.

Six weeks later, a third piece of news arrives. I am called out of the Hospital Ward, where I was lying wretchedly ill, to receive a special message from you through the Governor

of the Prison. He reads me out a letter you had addressed to him in which you stated that you proposed to publish an article 'on the case of Mr. Oscar Wilde', in the *Mercure de France*, (a 'magazine', you added for some extraordinary reason, 'corresponding to our *English Fortnightly Review*,') and were anxious to obtain my permission to publish extracts and selections from … what letters? The letters I had written to you from Holloway Prison! The letters that should have been to you things sacred and secret beyond anything in the whole world! These actually were the letters you proposed to publish for the jaded *décadent* to wonder at, for the greedy *feuilletoniste* to chronicle, for the little lions of the *Quartier Latin* to gape and mouth at. Had there been nothing in your own heart to cry out against so vulgar a sacrilege you might at least have remembered the sonnet he wrote who saw with such sorrow and scorn the letters of John Keats sold by public auction in London, and have understood at last the real meaning of my lines.

> '… I think they love not art
> Who break the crystal of a poet's heart
> That small and sickly eyes may glance or gloat.'

For what was your article to show? That I had been too fond of you? The Paris *gamin* was quite aware of the fact. They all read the newspapers, and most of them write for

them.... That I was a man of genius? The French understood that, and the peculiar quality of my genius, much better than you did, or could have been expected to do... That along with genius goes often a curious perversity of passion and desire? Admirable: but the subject belongs to Lombroso rather than to you. Besides the pathological phenomenon in question is also found amongst those who have not genius.... That in your war of hate with your Father I was at once shield and weapon to each of you? Nay more, that in that hideous hunt for my life, that took place when the war was over, he never could have reached me had not your nets been already about my feet? Quite true: but I am told that Henri Bauer had already done it extremely well. Besides to corroborate his view, had such been your intention, you did not require to publish my letters; at any rate those written from Holloway prison.

Will you say, in answer to my questions, that in one of my Holloway letters I had myself asked you to try as far as you were able, to set me a little right with some small portion of the world? Certainly, I did so. Remember how and why I am here, at this very moment. Do you think I am here on account of my relations with the witnesses on my trial? My relations, real or supposed, with people of that kind were matters of no interest to either the Government or Society. They knew nothing of them, and cared less. I am here for having tried to put your father into prison. My attempt

failed of course. My own counsel threw up their briefs. Your Father completely turned the tables on me, and had *me* in prison, has me there still. That is why there is contempt felt for me. That is why people despise me. That is why I have to serve out every day, every hour, every minute of my dreadful imprisonment. That is why my petitions have been refused.... You were the only person who, and without in any way exposing yourself to scorn or danger or blame, could have given another colour to the whole affair: have put the matter in a different light: have shown to a certain degree how things really stood. I would not of course have expected, nor indeed wished you to have stated how and for what purpose you had sought my assistance in your trouble at Oxford: or how, and for what purpose, if you had a purpose at all, you had practically never left my side for nearly three years. My incessant attempts to break off a friendship that was so ruinous to me as an artist, as a man of position, as a member of society even, need not have been chronicled with the accuracy with which they have been set down here. Nor would I have desired you to have described the scenes you used to make with such almost monotonous recurrence; nor to have reprinted your wonderful series of telegrams to me with their strange mixture of romance and finance; nor to have quoted from your letters the more revolting or heartless passages, as I have been forced to do. Still, I thought it would have been good, as well for you as for me, if you

De Profundis

had made some protest against your Father's version of our friendship, one no less grotesque than venomous, and as absurd in its reference to you as it was dishonouring in its reference to me. That version has now actually passed into serious history: it is quoted, believed, and chronicled: the preacher has taken it for his text, and the moralist for his barren theme: and I who appealed to all the ages have had to accept my verdict from one who is an ape and a buffoon. I have said, and with some bitterness, I admit, in this letter that such was the irony of things that your Father would live to be the hero of a Sunday-school tract: that you would rank with the infant Samuel: and that my place would be between Gilles de Retz and the Marquis de Sade. I dare say it is best so. I have no desire to complain. One of the many lessons that one learns in prison is that things are what they are, and will be what they will be. Nor have I any doubt but that the leper of mediaevalism, and the author of *Justine* will prove better company than Sandford and Merton. But at the time I wrote to you, I felt that for both our sakes it would be a good thing, a proper thing, a right thing *not* to accept the account your Father had put forward through his counsel for the edification of a Philistine world and that is why I asked you to think out and write something that would be nearer the Truth. It would at least have been better for you than scribbling to the French papers about the domestic life of your parents. What did the French care

79

whether or not your parents had led a happy domestic life? One cannot conceive a subject more entirely uninteresting to them. What did interest them was how an artist of my distinction, one who by the school and movement of which he was the incarnation had exercised a marked influence on the direction of French thought, could, having led such a life, have brought such an action. Had you proposed for your article to publish the letters, endless I fear in number, in which I had spoken to you of the ruin you were bringing on my life, of the madness of moods of rage that you were allowing to master you to your own hurt as well as to mine, and of my desire, nay my determination to end a friendship so fatal to me in every way, I could have understood it, though I would not have allowed such letters to be published: when your father's counsel desiring to catch me in a contradiction suddenly produced in Court a letter of mine, written to you in March '93, in which I stated that, rather than endure a repetition of the hideous scenes you seemed to take such a terrible pleasure in making, I would readily consent to be 'blackmailed by every renter in London', it was a very real grief to me that that side of my friendship with you should incidentally[,] be revealed to the common gaze: but that you should have been so slow to see, so lacking in all sensitiveness, and so dull in apprehension of what is rare, delicate and beautiful, as to propose yourself to publish the letters in which, and through which, I was trying to keep

alive the very spirit and soul of Love, that it might dwell in my body through the long years of that body's humiliation, – this was, and still is to me a source of the very deepest pain, the most poignant disappointment. Why you did so, I fear I know but too well. If Hate blinded your eyes, Vanity sewed your eyelids together with threads of iron. The faculty by which, and 'by which alone, one can under-stand others in their real as in their ideal relations', your narrow egotism had blunted, and long disuse had made of no avail. The imagination was as much in prison as I was. Vanity had barred-up the windows and the name of the warder was Hate.

All this took place in the early part of November of the year before last. A great river of life flows between you and a date so distant. Hardly, if at all, can you see across so wide a waste. But to me it seems to have occurred, I will not say yesterday, but today. Suffering is one long moment. We cannot divide it by seasons. We can only record its moods, and chronicle their return. With us time itself does not progress. It revolves. It seems to circle round one centre of pain. The paralysing immobility of a life, every circumstance of which is regulated after an unchangeable pattern, so that we eat and drink and walk and lie down and pray, or kneel at least for prayer, according to the inflexible laws of an iron formula: – this immobile quality, that makes each dreadful day in the very minutest detail like its brother, seems to

communicate itself to those external forces the very essence of whose existence is ceaseless change. Of seed-time or harvest; of the reapers bending over the corn, or the grape-gatherers threading through the vines; of the grass in the orchard made white with broken blossoms, or strewn with fallen fruit; of these we know nothing and can know nothing. For us there is only one season, the season of Sorrow. The very sun and moon seem taken from us. Outside, the day may be blue and gold, but the light that creeps down through the thickly-muffled glass of the small iron-barred window beneath which one sits is grey and niggard. It is always twilight in one's cell, as it [is] always midnight in one's heart. And in the sphere of thought, no less than in the sphere of time, motion is no more. The thing that you personally have long ago forgotten, or can easily forget, is happening to me now, and will happen to me again tomorrow. Remember this, and you will be able to understand a little of why I am writing to you, and in this manner writing.

A week later, I am transferred here. Three more months go over and my mother dies. You knew, none better, how deeply I loved and honoured her. Her death was so terrible to me that I, once a lord of language, have no words in which to express my anguish and my shame: never, even in the most perfect days of my development as an artist, could [I] have had words fit to bear so august a burden, or to move with sufficient stateliness of music through the purple

pageant of my incommunicable woe. She and my Father
had bequeathed me a name they had made noble and
honoured not merely in Literature, Art, Archaeology and
Science, but in the public history of my own country in its
evolution as a nation. I had disgraced that name eternally.
I had made it a low byword among low people. I had dragged
it through the very mire. I had given it to brutes that they
might make it brutal, and to fools that they might turn it
into a synonym for folly. What I suffered then, and still
suffer, is not for pen to write or paper to record. My wife,
at that time kind and gentle to me, rather than that I should
hear the news from indifferent lips, travelled, ill as she was,
all the way from Genoa to England to break to me herself
the tidings of so irreparable, so irredeemable, a loss. Messages
of sympathy reached me from all who had still affection for
me. Even people who had not known me personally, hearing
what a new sorrow had come into my broken life, wrote to
ask that some expression of their condolence should be
conveyed to me. You alone stood aloof, sent me no message,
and wrote me no letter. Of such actions, it is best to say
what Virgil says to Dante of those whose lives have been
barren in noble impulse and shallow of intention: '*non
ragioniam di lor, ma guarda e parsa.*'

Three months go over. The calendar of my daily conduct
and labour that hangs on the outside of my cell-door, with
my name and sentence written upon it, tells me that it is

May-time. My friends come to see me again. I enquire, as I always do, after you. I am told that you are in your villa at Naples, and are bringing out a volume of poems. At the close of the interview it is mentioned casually that you are dedicating them to me. The tidings seemed to give me a sort of nausea of life. I said nothing, but silently went back to my cell with contempt and scorn in my heart. How could you dream of dedicating a volume of poems to me without first asking my permission? Dream, do I say? How could you dare to do such a thing? Will you give as your answer that in my days of greatness and fame I had consented to receive the dedication of your early work? Certainly, I did so; just as I would have accepted the homage of any other young man beginning the difficult and beautiful art of literature. All homage is delightful to an artist, and doubly sweet when youth brings it. Laurel and bay leaf wither when aged hands pluck them. Only youth has a right to crown an artist. That is the real privilege of being young, if youth only knew it. But the days of abasement and infamy are different from those of greatness and of fame. You have yet to learn that Prosperity, Pleasure and Success may be rough of grain and common in fibre, but that Sorrow is the most sensitive of all created things. There is nothing that stirs in the whole world of thought or motion to which sorrow does not vibrate in terrible if exquisite pulsation. The thin beaten-out leaf of tremulous gold that chronicles the

direction of forces that the eye cannot see is in comparison coarse. It is a wound that bleeds when any hand but that of Love touches it and even then must bleed again, though not in pain. You could write to the Governor of Wandsworth Prison to ask my permission to publish my letters in the *Mercure de France*, 'corresponding to our *English Fortnightly Review*'. Why not have written to the Governor of the Prison at Reading to ask my permission to dedicate your poems to me, whatever fantastic description you may have chosen to give of them? Was it because in the one case the magazine in question had been prohibited by me from publishing letters the legal copyright of which, as you are of course perfectly well aware, was and is vested entirely in me, and in the other you thought that you could enjoy the wilfulness of your own way without my knowing anything about it till it was too late to interfere? The mere fact that I was a man disgraced, ruined, and in prison should have made you, if you desired to write my name on the fore-page of your work, beg it of me as a favour, an honour, a privilege. That is the way in which one should approach those who are in distress and sit in shame. Where there is Sorrow there is holy ground. Some day people will realise what that means. You will know nothing of life till you do. Robbie, and natures like his, can realise it. When I was brought down from my prison to the Court of Bankruptcy, between two policemen, Robbie waited in the long dreary corridor, that before the

whole crowd, whom an action so sweet and simple hushed into silence, he might gravely raise his hat to me, as handcuffed and with bowed head I passed him by. Men have gone to heaven for smaller things than that. It was in this spirit, and with this mode of love, that the saints knelt down to wash the feet of the poor, or stooped to kiss the leper on the cheek. I have never said one single word to him about what he did. I do not know to the present moment whether he is aware that I was even conscious of his action. It is not a thing for which one can render formal thanks in formal words. I store it in the Treasury-house of my heart. I keep it there as a secret debt that I am glad to think I can never possibly repay. It is embalmed and kept sweet by the myrrh and cassia of many tears. When Wisdom has been profitless to me, and Philosophy barren, and the proverbs and phrases of those who have sought to give me consolation as dust and ashes in my mouth, the memory of that little lovely silent act of Love has unsealed for me all the wells of pity, made the desert blossom like a rose, and brought me out of the bitterness of lonely exile into harmony with the wounded, broken and great heart of the world. When you are able to understand, not merely how beautiful Robbie's action was, but why it meant so much to me, and always will mean so much, then, perhaps, you will realise how and in what spirit you should have approached me for permission to dedicate to me your verses.

De Profundis

It is only right to state, that in any case, I would not have accepted the dedication. Though, possibly, it would under other circumstances have pleased me to have been asked, I would have refused the request for *your* sake, irrespective of any feelings of my own. The first volume of poems that in the very springtime of his manhood a young man sends forth to the world should be like a blossom or flower of spring, like the whitethorn in the meadow at Magdalen, or the cowslips in the Cumnor fields. It should not be burdened by the weight of a terrible, a revolting tragedy, a terrible, a revolting scandal. If I had allowed my name to serve as herald to the book It would have been a grave artistic error. It would have brought a wrong atmosphere round the whole work, and in modern art atmosphere counts for so much. Modern life is complex and relative. Those are its two distinguishing notes. To render the first we require atmosphere with its subtlety of *nuances*, of suggestion, of strange perspectives: as for the second we require background. That is why Sculpture has ceased to be a representative art; and why Music *is* a representative art; and why Literature is, and has been, and always will remain the supreme representative art. Your little book should have brought with it Sicilian and Arcadian airs, not the pestilent foulness of the criminal dock or the close breath of the convict cell. Nor would such a dedication as you proposed have been merely an error of taste in Art; it would from other points of view have been entirely unseemly.

It would have looked like a continuance of your conduct before and after my arrest. It would have given people the impression of being an attempt at foolish bravado: an example of that kind of courage that is sold cheap and bought cheap in the streets of shame. As far as our friendship is concerned Nemesis has crushed us both like flies. The dedication of verses to me when I was in prison would have seemed a sort of silly effort at smart repartee, an accomplishment on which in your old days of dreadful letter-writing – days never, I sincerely hope for your sake, to return – you used openly to pride yourself and about which it was your joy to boast. It would not have produced the serious, the beautiful effect which I trust – I believe indeed – you had intended. Had you consulted me, I would have advised you to delay the publication of your verses for a little; or, if that proved displeasing to you, to publish anonymously at first, and then when you had won lovers by your song – the only sort of lovers really worth the winning – you might have turned round and said to the world 'These flowers that you admire are of my sowing, and now I offer them to one whom you regard as a pariah and an outcast, as my tribute to what I love and reverence and admire in him'. But you chose the wrong method and the wrong moment. There is a tact in love, and a tact in literature: you were not sensitive to either.

I have spoken to you at length on this point in order that you should grasp Its full bearings, and understand why I

wrote at once to Robbie in terms of such scorn and contempt
of you, and absolutely prohibited the dedication, and desired
that the words I had written of you should be copied out
carefully and sent to you. I felt that at last the time had
come when you should be made to see, to recognise, to
realise a little of what you had done. Blindness may be
carried so far that it becomes grotesque, and an unimaginative
nature, if something be not done to rouse it, will become
petrified into absolute insensibility, so that while the body
may eat, and drink, and have its pleasures, the soul, whose
house it is, may, like the soul of Branca d'Oria in Dante, be
dead absolutely. My letter seems to have arrived not a
moment too soon. It fell on you, as far as I can judge, like
a thunderbolt. You describe yourself, in your answer to
Robbie, as being 'deprived of all power of thought and
expression'. Indeed, apparently, you can think of nothing
better than to write to your mother to complain. Of course,
she, with that blindness to your real good that has been her
ill-starred fortune and yours, gives you every comfort she
can think of, and lulls you back, I suppose, into your former
unhappy, unworthy condition; while as far as I am concerned,
she lets my friends know that she is 'very much annoyed' at
the severity of my remarks about you. Indeed it is not merely
to my friends that she conveys her sentiments of annoyance,
but also to those – a very much larger number, I need hardly
remind you – who are not my friends: and I am informed

now, and through channels very kindly-disposed to you and yours, that in consequence of this a great deal of the sympathy that, by reason of my distinguished genius and terrible sufferings, had been gradually but surely growing up for me, has been entirely taken away. People say 'Ah! He first tried to get the kind father put into prison and failed: now he turns round and blames the innocent son for his failure. How right we were to despise him! How worthy of contempt he is!' It seems to me that, when my name is mentioned in your mother's presence, if she has no word of sorrow or regret for her share – no slight one – in the ruin of my house, it would be more seemly if she remained silent. And as for you – don't you think now that, instead of writing to *her* to complain, it would have been better for you, in every way, to have written to *me* directly, and to have had the courage to say to me whatever you had or fancied you had to say? It is nearly a year ago now since I wrote that letter. You cannot have remained during that entire time 'deprived of all power of thought and expression'. Why did you not write to me? You saw by my letter how deeply wounded, how outraged I was by your whole conduct. More than that; you saw your entire friendship with me set before you, at last, in its true light, and by a mode not to be mistaken. Often in old days I had told you that you were ruining my life. You had always laughed. When Edwin Levy at the very beginning of our friendship, seeing your manner

of putting me forward to bear the brunt, and annoyance, and expense even of that unfortunate Oxford mishap of yours, if we must so term it, in reference to which his advice and help had been sought, warned me for the space of a whole hour against knowing you, you laughed, as at Bracknell I described to you my long and impressive interview with him. When I told you how even that unfortunate young man who ultimately stood beside me in the Dock had warned me more than once that you would prove far more fatal in bringing me to utter destruction than any even of the common lads whom I was foolish enough to know, you laughed, though not with such sense of amusement. When my more prudent or less well-disposed friends either warned me, or left me, on account of my friendship with you, you laughed with scorn. You laughed immoderately when, on the occasion of your Father writing his first abusive letter to you about me, I told you that I knew I would be the mere catspaw of your dreadful quarrel and come to some evil between you. But every single thing had happened as I had said it would happen, as far as the result goes. You had no excuse for not seeing how all things had come to pass. Why did you not write to me? Was it cowardice? Was it callousness? What was it? The fact that I was outraged with you, and had expressed my sense of the outrage, was all the more reason for writing. If you thought my letter just, you should have written. If you thought it in the smallest point

unjust, you should have written. I waited for a letter. I felt sure that at last you would see that, if old affection, much-protested love, the thousand acts of ill requited kindness I had showered on you, the thousand unpaid debts of gratitude you owed me: – that if all these were nothing to you, mere duty itself, most barren of all bonds between man and man, should have made you write. You cannot say that you seriously thought I was obliged to receive none but business communications from members of my family. You knew perfectly well that every twelve weeks Robbie was writing to me a little budget of literary news. Nothing can be more charming than his letters, in their wit, their clever concentrated criticism, their light touch: they are real letters: they are like a person talking to one: they have the quality of a French *causerie intime*: and in his delicate modes of deference to me, appealing at one time to my judgment, at another to my sense of humour, at another to my instinct for beauty or to my culture, and reminding me in a hundred subtle ways that once I was to many an arbiter of style in Art, the supreme arbiter to some, he shows how he has the tact of love as well as the tact of literature. His letters have been the little messengers between me and that beautiful unreal world of Art where once I was King, and would have remained King, indeed, had I not let myself be lured into the imperfect world of coarse uncompleted passions, of appetite without distinction, desire without limit, and

formless greed. Yet, when all is said, surely you might have been able to understand, or conceive, at any rate, in your own mind, that, even on the ordinary grounds of mere psychological curiosity, it would have been more interesting to me to hear from *you* than to learn that Alfred Austin was trying to bring out a volume of poems, or that Street was writing dramatic criticisms for the Daily Chronicle, or that by one who cannot speak a panegyric without stammering Mrs Meynell had been pronounced to be the new Sibyl of Style? Ah! Had *you* been in prison – I will not say through any fault of mine, for that would be a thought too terrible for me to bear – but through fault of your own, error of your own, faith in some unworthy friend, slip in sensual mire, trust misapplied, or love ill-bestowed, or none, or all of these – do you think that I would have allowed you to eat your heart away in darkness and solitude without trying in some way, however slight, to help you to bear the bitter burden of your disgrace? Do you think that I would not have let you know that if you suffered, I was suffering too: that if you wept, there were tears in my eyes also: and that if you lay in the house of bondage and were despised of men, I out of my very griefs had built a house in which to dwell until your coming, a treasury in which all that men had denied to you would be laid up for your healing, one hundredfold in increase? If bitter necessity, or prudence, to *me* more bitter still, had prevented my being near you, and

robbed me of the joy of your presence, though seen through prison-bars and in a shape of shame, I would have written to you in season and out of season in the hope that some mere phrase, some single word, some broken echo even of Love might reach you. If you had refused to receive my letters, I would have written none the less, so that you should have known that at any rate there were always letters waiting for you. Many have done so to me. Every three months people write to me, or propose to write to me. Their letters and communications are kept. They will be handed to me when I go out of prison. I know that they are there. I know the names of the people who have written them. I know that they are full of sympathy, and affection, and kindness. That is sufficient for me. I need to know no more. Your silence has been horrible. Nor has it been a silence of weeks and months merely, but of years; of years even as they have to count them who, like yourself, live swiftly in happiness and can hardly catch the gilt feet of the days as they dance by, and are out of breath in the chase after pleasure. It is a silence without excuse; a silence without palliation. I knew you had feet of clay. Who knew it better? When I wrote, among my aphorisms, that it was simply the feet of clay that made the gold of the image precious, it was of you I was thinking. But it is no gold image with clay feet that you have made of yourself. Out of the very dust of the common highway that the hooves of horned things pash

into mire you have moulded your perfect semblance for me to look at, so that, whatever my secret desire might have been, it would be impossible for me now to have for you any feeling other than that of contempt and scorn, for myself any feeling other than that of contempt and scorn either. And, setting aside all other reasons, your indifference, your worldly wisdom, your callousness, your prudence, whatever you may choose to call it, has been made doubly bitter to me by the peculiar circumstances that either accompanied or followed my fall. Other miserable men, when they are thrown into prison, if they are robbed of the beauty of the world, are at least safe, in some measure, from the world's most deadly slings, most awful arrows. They can hide in the darkness of their cells, and of their very disgrace make a mode of sanctuary. The world, having had its will, goes its way, and they are left to suffer undisturbed. With me it has been different. Sorrow after sorrow has come beating at the prison doors in search of me. They have opened the gates wide and let them in. Hardly, if at all, have my friends been suffered to see me. But my enemies have had full access to me always. Twice in my public appearances at the Bankruptcy Court, twice again in my public transferences from one prison to another, have I been shown under conditions of unspeakable humiliation to the gaze and mockery of men. The messenger of Death has brought me his tidings and gone his way, and in entire solitude, and

isolated from all that could give me comfort, or suggest relief, I have had to bear the intolerable burden of misery and remorse that the memory of my mother placed upon me, and places on me still. Hardly has that wound been dulled, not healed, by time, when violent and bitter and harsh letters come to me from my wife through her solicitor. I am, at once, taunted and threatened with poverty. That I can bear. I can school myself to worse than that. But my two children are taken from me by legal procedure. That is and always will remain to me a source of infinite distress, of infinite pain, of grief without end or limit. That the law should decide, and take upon itself to decide that I am one unfit to be with my own children is something quite horrible to me. The disgrace of prison is as nothing compared to it. I envy the other men who tread the yard along with me. I am sure that their children wait for them, look for their coming, will be sweet to them.

The poor are wiser, more charitable, more kind, more sensitive than we are. In their eyes prison is a tragedy in a man's life, a misfortune, a casualty, something that calls for sympathy in others. They speak of one who is in prison as of one who is 'in trouble' simply. It is the phrase they always use, and the expression has the perfect wisdom of Love in it. With people of our rank it is different. With us prison makes a man a pariah. I, and such as I am, have hardly any right to air and sun. Our presence taints the

pleasures of others. We are unwelcome when we reappear. To revisit the glimpses of the moon is not for us. Our very children are taken away. Those lovely links with humanity are broken. We are doomed to be solitary, while our sons still live. We are denied the one thing that might heal us and help us, that might bring balm to the bruised heart, and peace to the soul in pain. And to all this has been added the hard, small fact that by your actions and by your silence, by what you have done and by what you have left undone, you have made every day of my long imprisonment still more difficult for me to live through. The very bread and water of prison fare you have by your conduct changed. You have rendered the one bitter and the other brackish to me. The sorrow you should have shared you have doubled, the pain you should have sought to lighten you have quickened to anguish. I have no doubt that you did not mean to do so. I know that you did not mean to do so. It was simply that 'one really fatal defect of your character, your entire lack of imagination.'

And the end of it all is that I have got to forgive you. I must do so. I don't write this letter to put bitterness into your heart, but to pluck it out of mine. For my own sake I must forgive you. One cannot always keep an adder in one's breast to feed on one, nor rise up every night to sow thorns in the garden of one's soul. It will not be difficult at all for me to do so, if you help me a little. Whatever

you did to me in old days I always readily forgave. It did you no good then. Only one whose life is without stain of any kind can forgive sins. But now when I sit in humiliation and disgrace it is different. My forgiveness should mean a great deal to you now. Some day you will realise it. Whether you do so early or late, soon or not at all, my way is clear before me. I cannot allow you to go through life bearing in your heart the burden of having ruined a man like me. The thought might make you callously indifferent, or morbidly sad. I must take the burden from you and put it on my own shoulders. I must say to myself that neither you nor your Father, multiplied a thousand times over, could possibly have ruined a man like me: that I ruined myself: and that nobody, great or small, can be ruined except by his own hand. I am quite ready to do so. I am trying to do so, though you may not think it at the present moment. If I have brought this pitiless indictment against you, think what an indictment I bring without pity against myself. Terrible as what you did to me was, what I did to myself was far more terrible still. I was a man who stood in symbolic relations to the art and culture of my age. I had realised this for myself at the very dawn of my manhood, and had forced my age to realise it afterwards. Few men hold such a position in their own lifetime, and have it so acknowledged. It is usually discerned, if discerned at all, by the historian, or the critic, long after both the

man and his age have passed away. With me it was different. I felt it myself, and made others feel it. Byron was a symbolic figure, but his relations were to the passion of his age and its weariness of passion. Mine were to something more noble, more permanent, of more vital issue, of larger scope. The Gods had given me almost everything. I had genius, a distinguished name, high social position, brilliancy, intellectual daring: I made art a philosophy, and philosophy an art: I altered the minds of men and the colours of things: there was nothing I said or did that did not make people wonder: I took the drama, the most objective form known to art, and made it as personal a mode of expression as the lyric or the sonnet, at the same time that I widened its range and enriched its characterisation: drama, novel, poem in rhyme, poem in prose, subtle or fantastic dialogue, whatever I touched I made beautiful in a new mode of beauty: to truth itself I gave what is false no less than what is true as its rightful province, and showed that the false and the true are merely forms of intellectual existence: I treated Art as the supreme reality, and life as a mere mode of fiction: I awoke the imagination of my century so that it created myth and legend around me: I summed up all systems in a phrase, and all existence in an epigram. Along with these things, I had things that were different. I let myself be lured into long spells of senseless and sensual ease. I amused myself with being a *flâneur*, a dandy, a man

of fashion. I surrounded myself with the smaller natures and the meaner minds. I became the spendthrift of my own genius, and to waste an eternal youth gave me a curious joy. Tired of being on the heights I deliberately went to the depths in the search for new sensation. What the paradox was to me in the sphere of thought, perversity became to me in the sphere of passion. Desire, at the end, was a malady, or a madness, or both. I grew careless of the lives of others. I took pleasure where it pleased me, and passed on. I forgot that every little action of the common day makes or unmakes character, and that therefore what one has done in the secret chamber one has someday to cry aloud on the housetop. I ceased to be Lord over myself. I was no longer the captain of my Soul, and did not know it. I allowed you to dominate me. and your father to frighten me. I ended in horrible disgrace. There is only one thing for me now, absolute Humility; just as there is only one thing for you, absolute Humility also. You had better come down into the dust and learn it beside me. I have lain in prison for nearly two years. Out of my nature has come wild despair; an abandonment to grief that was piteous even to look at; terrible and impotent rage; bitterness and scorn; anguish that wept aloud, misery that could find no voice, sorrow that was dumb. I have passed through every possible mood of suffering. Better than Wordsworth himself I know what Wordsworth meant when he said,

De Profundis

'Suffering is permanent, obscure, and dark
And has the nature of Infinity.'

But while there were times when I rejoiced in the idea that
my sufferings were to be endless, I could not bear them to
be without meaning. Now I find hidden away in my nature
something that tells me that nothing in the whole world is
meaningless, and suffering least of all. That something hidden
away in my nature, like a treasure in a field, is Humility.

It is the last thing left in me, and the best: the ultimate
discovery at which I have arrived, the starting point for a
fresh development. It has come to me right out of myself,
so I know that it has come at the proper time. It could not
have come before, nor later. Had anyone told me of it, I
would have rejected it. Had it been brought to me, I would
have refused it. As I found it, I want to keep it. I must do
so. It is the one thing that has in it the elements of life, of
a new life, a *Vita Nuova* for me. Of all things it is the
strangest. One cannot acquire it, except by surrendering
everything that one has. It is only when one has lost all
things, that one knows that one possesses it.

Now that I realise that it is in me, I see quite clearly what
I have got to do, what, in fact, I must do. And when I use
such a phrase as that, I need not tell you that I am not
alluding to any external sanction or command. I admit none.
I am far more of an individualist than I ever was. Nothing

seems to me of the smallest value except what one gets out of oneself. My nature is seeking a fresh mode of self-realisation. That is all I am concerned with. And the first thing that I have got to do is to free myself from any possible bitterness of feeling against you. I am completely penniless, and absolutely homeless. Yet there are worse things in the world than that. I am quite candid when I tell you that rather than go out from this prison with bitterness in my heart against the world, I would gladly and readily beg my bread from door to door. If I got nothing from the house of the rich, I would get something at the house of the poor. Those who have much are often greedy. Those who have little always share. I would not a bit mind sleeping in the cool grass in summer, and when winter came on sheltering myself by the warm close-thatched rick, or under the penthouse of a great barn, provided I had love in my heart. The external things of life seem to me now of no importance at all. You can see to what intensity of individualism I have arrived – or am arriving rather, for the journey is long, and 'where I walk there are thorns'. Of course I know that to ask for alms on the highway is not to be my lot, and that if ever I lie in the cool grass at night-time it will be to write sonnets to the moon. When I go out of prison, Robbie will be waiting for me on the other side of the big iron-studded gate, and he is the symbol not merely of his own affection, but of the affection of many others besides. I believe I am

to have enough to live on for about eighteen months at any rate, so that if I may not write beautiful books, I may at least read beautiful books; and what joy can be greater? After that, I hope to be able to recreate my creative faculty. But were things different: had I not a friend left in the world: were there not a single house open to me in pity: had I to accept the wallet and ragged cloak of sheer penury: as long as I still remained free from all resentment, hardness, and scorn, I would be able to face the life with much more calm and confidence than I would were my body in purple and fine linen, and the soul within it sick with hate. And I shall really have no difficulty in forgiving you. But to make it a pleasure for me you must feel that you want it. When you really want it you will find it waiting for you.

I need not say that my task does not end there. It would be comparatively easy, if it did. There is much more before me. I have hills far steeper to climb, valleys much darker to pass through. And I have to get it all out of myself. Neither Religion, Morality, nor Reason can help me at all.

Morality does not help me. I am a born antinomian. I am one of those who are made for exceptions, not for laws. But while I see that there is nothing wrong in what one does, I see that there is something wrong in what one becomes. It is well to have learned that. Religion does not help me. The faith that others give to what is unseen, I give to what one can touch, and look at. My Gods dwell in temples made

with hands, and within the circle of actual experience is my creed made perfect and complete: too complete it may be, for like many or all of those who have placed their Heaven in this earth, I have found in it not merely the beauty of Heaven, but the horror of Hell also. When I think about Religion at all, I feel as if I would like to found an order for those who cannot believe: the Confraternity of the Faithless one might call it, where on an altar, on which no taper burned, a priest, in whose heart peace had no dwelling, might celebrate with unblessed bread and a chalice empty of wine. Every thing to be true must become a religion. And agnosticism should have its ritual no less than faith. It has sown its martyrs, it should reap its saints, and praise God daily for having hidden Himself from man. But whether it be faith or agnosticism, it must be nothing external to me. Its symbols must be of my own creating. Only that is spiritual which makes its own form. If I may not find its secret within myself, I shall never find it. If I have not got it already, it will never come to me. Reason does not help me. It tells me that the laws under which I am convicted are wrong and unjust laws, and the system under which I have suffered a wrong and unjust system. But, somehow, I have got to make both of these things just and right to me. And, exactly as in Art one is only concerned with what a particular thing is at a particular moment to oneself, so it is also in the ethical evolution of one's character. I have got to make everything that has

De Profundis

happened to me good for me. The plank-bed, the loathsome food, the hard ropes shredded into oakum till one's finger-tips grow dull with pain, the menial offices with which each day begins and finishes, the harsh orders that routine seems to necessitate, the dreadful dress that makes sorrow grotesque to look at, the silence, the solitude, the shame: each and all of these things I have to transform into a spiritual experience. There is not a single degradation of the body which I must not try and make into a spiritualising of the soul. I want to get to the point when I shall be able to say quite simply and without affectation that the two great turning points in my life were when my Father sent me to Oxford, and when society sent me to prison. I will not say that prison is the best thing that could have happened to me, for that phrase would savour of too great bitterness towards myself. I would sooner say, or hear it said of me, that I was so typical a child of my age, that in my perversity, and for that perversity's sake, I turned the good things of my life to evil, and the evil things of my life to good. What is said, however, by myself or by others matters little. The important thing, the thing that lies before me, the thing that I have to do, or be for the brief remainder of my days one maimed, marred, and incomplete, is to absorb into my nature all that has been done to me, to make it part of me, to accept it without complaint, fear, or reluctance. The supreme vice is shallowness. Whatever is realised is right.

When first I was put into prison some people advised me to try and forget who I was. It was ruinous advice. It is only by realising what I am, that I have found comfort of any kind. Now I am advised by others to try on my release to forget that I have ever been in a prison at all. I know that would be equally fatal. It would mean that I would be always haunted by an intolerable sense of disgrace, and that those things that are meant as much for me as for anyone else, the beauty of the sun and the moon, the pageant of the seasons, the music of daybreak and the silence of great nights, the rain falling through the leaves, or the dew creeping over the grass and making it silver, would all be tainted for me, and lose their healing power and their power of communicating joy. To regret one's own experiences is to arrest one's own development. To deny one's own experiences is to put a lie into the lips of one's own life. It is no less than a denial of the soul. For just as the body absorbs things of all kinds, things common and unclean no less than those that the priest or a vision has cleansed, and converts them into swiftness or strength, into the play of beautiful muscles and the moulding of fair flesh, into the curves and colours of the hair, the lips, the eye: so the soul, in its turn, has its nutritive functions also, and can transform into noble moods of thought, and passions of high import, what in itself is base, cruel, and degrading: nay more, may find in these its most august modes of assertion, and can often reveal itself

most perfectly through what was intended to desecrate or destroy. The fact of my having been the common prisoner of a common gaol I must frankly accept, and, curious as it may seem to you, one of the things I shall have to teach myself is not to be ashamed of it. I must accept it as a punishment, and if one is ashamed of having been punished, one might just as well never have been punished at all. Of course there are many things of which I was convicted that I had not done, but then there are many things of which I was convicted that I had done, and a still greater number of things in my life for which I never was indicted at all. I have said in this letter, that the Gods are strange, and punish us for what is good and humane in us as much as for what is evil and perverse, – I must accept the fact that one is punished for the good as well as for the evil that one does. I have no doubt that it is quite right one should be. It helps one, or should help one, to realise both, and not to be too conceited about either. And if I then am not ashamed of my punishment, as I hope not to be, I shall be able to think, and walk, and live with freedom. Many men on their release carry their prison along with them into the air, hide it as a secret disgrace in their hearts, and at length like poor poisoned things creep into some hole and die. It is wretched that they should have to do so, and it is wrong – terribly wrong, of Society that it should force them to do so. Society takes upon itself the right to inflict appalling punishment

on the individual, but it also has the supreme vice of shallowness, and fails to realise what it has done. When the man's punishment is over, it leaves him to himself: that is to say it abandons him at the very moment when its highest duty towards him begins. It is really ashamed of its own actions, and shuns those whom it has punished, as people shun a creditor whose debt they cannot pay, or one on whom they have inflicted an irreparable, an irredeemable wrong. I claim on my side that if I realise what I have suffered, Society should realise what it has inflicted on me; and that there should be no bitterness or hate on either side. Of course I know that from one point of view things will be made more difficult for me than for others, must indeed, by the very nature of the case, be made so. The poor thieves and outcasts who are imprisoned here with me are in many respects more fortunate than I am. The little way in grey city or green field that saw their sin is small: to find those who know nothing of what they have done they need go no further than a bird might fly between the twilight before dawn and dawn itself: but for me 'the world is shrivelled to a handsbreadth', and everywhere I turn my name is written on the rocks in lead. For I have come, not from obscurity into the momentary notoriety of crime, but from a sort of eternity of fame to a sort of eternity of infamy, and sometimes seem to myself to have shown, if indeed it required showing, that between the famous and the infamous there is but one step, if so much as one. Still in the very fact that people will recognise me wherever I go, and know all about my life, as far as its follies go, I can discern something good for me. It will force on me the necessity of again asserting myself as an artist, and as soon as I possibly can. If I can produce even one more beautiful work of art I shall be able to rob malice of its venom, and cowardice of its sneer, and to pluck out the tongue of scorn by the roots. And if life be, as it surely is, a problem to me, I am no less a problem to Life. People must adopt some attitude towards me, and so pass judgment both on themselves and me. I need not say I am not talking of particular individuals. The only people I would care to be with now are artists and people who have suffered: those who know what Beauty is, and those who know what Sorrow is: nobody else interests me. Nor am I making any demands on Life. In all that I have said I am simply concerned with my own mental attitude towards life as a whole; and I feel that not to be ashamed of having been punished is one of the first points I must attain to, for the sake of my own perfection, and because I am so imperfect.

Then I must learn how to be happy. Once I knew it, or thought I knew it, or thought I knew it, by instinct. It was always springtime once in my heart. My temperament was akin to joy. I filled my life to the very brim with pleasure, as one might fill a cup to the very brim with wine. Now I am approaching life from a completely new standpoint, and

even to conceive happiness is often extremely difficult for me. I remember during my first term at Oxford reading in Pater's *Renaissance* – that book which has had such a strange influence over my life – how Dante places low in the Inferno those who wilfully live in sadness, and going to the College Library and turning to the passage in the *Divine Comedy* where beneath the dreary marsh lie those who were 'sullen in the sweet air,' saying for ever through their sighs,

> 'Tristi fummo
> Nell' aer dolce che dal sol s'allegra.'

I knew the church condemned *accidia*, but the whole idea seemed to me quite fantastic, just the sort of sin, I fancied, a priest who knew nothing about real life would invent. Nor could I understand how Dante who says that 'sorrow remarries us to God' could have been so harsh to those who were enamoured of melancholy, if any such there really were. I had no idea that someday this would become to me one of the greatest temptations of my life. While I was in Wandsworth prison I longed to die. It was my one desire. When after two months in the Infirmary I was transferred here, and found myself growing gradually better in physical health, I was filled with rage. I determined to commit suicide on the very day on which I left prison. After a time that evil mood passed away, and I made up my mind to live, but to wear gloom as

a King wears purple: never to smile again: to turn whatever house I entered into a house of mourning: to make my friends walk slowly in sadness with me: to teach them that melancholy is the true secret of life: to maim them with an alien sorrow: to mar them with my own pain. Now I feel quite differently. I see it would be both ungrateful and unkind of me to pull so long a face that when my friends came to see me they would have to make their faces still longer in order to show their sympathy, or, if I desired to entertain them, to invite them to sit down silently to bitter herbs and funeral baked meats. I must learn how to be cheerful and happy. The last two occasions on which I was allowed to see my friends here, I tried to be as cheerful as possible, and to show my cheerfulness in order to make them some slight return for their trouble in coming all the way from town to visit me. It is only a slight return, I know, but it is the one, I feel certain, that pleases them most. I saw Robbie for an hour on Saturday week, and I tried to give the fullest possible expression of the delight I really felt at our meeting. And that, in the views and ideas I am here shaping for myself, I am quite right is shown to me by the fact that now for the first time since my imprisonment I have a real desire to live. There is before me so much to do, that I would regard it as a terrible tragedy if I died before I was allowed to complete at any rate a little of it. I see new developments in Art and Life, each one of which is a fresh mode of perfection. I long to live so that I

can explore what is no less than a new world to me! Do you want to know what this new world is? I think you can guess what it is. It is the world in which I have been living.

Sorrow, then, and all that it teaches one, is my new world. I used to live entirely for pleasure. I shunned sorrow and suffering of every kind. I hated both. I resolved to ignore them as far as possible: to treat them, that is to say, as modes of imperfection. They were not part of my scheme of life. They had no place in my philosophy. My mother, who knew life as a whole, used often to quote to me Goethe's lines – written by Carlyle in a book he had given her years ago, and translated I fancy, by him also:

> 'Who never ate his bread in sorrow,
> Who never spent the midnight hours
> Weeping and waiting for the morrow, –
> He knows you not, ye Heavenly Powers.'

They were the lines which that noble Queen of Prussia, whom Napoleon treated with such coarse brutality, used to quote in her humiliation and exile: they were the lines my mother often quoted in the troubles of her later life: I absolutely declined to accept or admit the enormous truth hidden in them. I could not understand it. I remember quite well how I used to tell her that I did not want to eat my bread in sorrow, or to pass any night weeping and watching

for a more bitter dawn. I had no idea that it was one of the special things that the Fates had in store for me; that for a whole year of my life, indeed, I was to do little else. But so has my portion been meted out to me; and during the last few months I have, after terrible struggles and difficulties, been able to comprehend some of the lessons hidden in the heart of pain. Clergymen, and people who use phrases without wisdom sometimes talk of suffering as a mystery. It is really a revelation. One discerns things that one never discerned before. One approaches the whole of history from a different standpoint. What one had felt dimly, through instinct, about Art, is intellectually and emotionally realised with perfect clearness of vision and absolute intensity of apprehension. I now see that sorrow, being the supreme emotion of which man is capable, is at once the type and test of all great Art. What the artist is always looking for is that mode of existence in which soul and body are one and indivisible: in which the outward is expressive of the inward: in which Form reveals. Of such modes of existence there are not a few: youth and the arts preoccupied with youth may serve as a model for us at one moment: at another, we may like to think that, in its subtlety and sensitiveness of impression, its suggestion of a spirit dwelling in external things and making its raiment of earth and air, of mist and city alike, and in the morbid sympathy of its moods, and tones and colours, modern landscape art is realising for us

pictorially what was realised in such plastic perfection by the Greeks: Music, in which all subject is absorbed in expression and cannot be separated from it, is a complex example, and a flower or a child a simple example, of what I mean: but Sorrow is the ultimate type both in life and Art. Behind Joy and Laughter there may be a temperament, coarse, hard and callous. But behind Sorrow there is always sorrow. Pain, unlike Pleasure, wears no mask. Truth in Art is not any correspondence between the essential idea and the accidental existence; it is not the resemblance of shape to shadow, or of the form mirrored in the crystal to the form itself: it is no Echo coming from a hollow hill, any more than it is the well of silver water in the valley that shows the moon to the moon and Narcissus to Narcissus. Truth in Art is the unity of a thing with itself: the outward rendered expressive of the inward: the soul made incarnate: the body instinct with spirit. For this reason there is no truth comparable to Sorrow. There are times when Sorrow seems to me to be the only truth. Other things may be illusions of the eye or the appetite, made to blind the one and cloy the other, but out of Sorrow have the worlds been built, and at the birth of a child or a star there is pain. More than this there is about Sorrow an intense, an extraordinary reality. I have said of myself that I was one who stood in symbolic relations to the art and culture of my age. There is not a single wretched man in this wretched place along with me who does not

stand in symbolic relations to the very secret of life. For the
secret of life is suffering. It is what is hidden behind
everything. When we begin to live, what is sweet is so sweet
to us, and what is bitter so bitter, that we inevitably direct
all our desires towards pleasure, and seek not merely for 'a
month or twain to feed on honeycomb,' but for all our years
to taste no other food, ignorant the while that we may be
really starving the soul. I remember talking once on this
subject to one of the most beautiful personalities I have ever
known: a woman, whose sympathy and noble kindness to
me both before and since the tragedy of my imprisonment
have been beyond power of description; one who has really
assisted me, though she does not know it, to bear the burden
of my troubles more than anyone else in the whole world
has: and all through the mere fact of her existence: through
her being what she is, partly an ideal and partly an influence,
a suggestion of what one might become, as well as a real
help towards becoming it, a soul that renders the common
air sweet, and makes what is spiritual seem as simple and
natural as sunlight or the sea, one for whom Beauty and
Sorrow walk hand in hand, and have the same message. On
the occasion of which I am thinking I recall distinctly how
I said to her that there was enough suffering in one narrow
London lane to show that God did not love man, and that
wherever there was any sorrow, though but that of a child,
in some little garden weeping over a fault that it had or had

not committed, the whole face of creation was completely marred. I was entirely wrong. She told me so, but I could not believe her. I was not in the sphere in which such belief was to be attained to. Now it seems to me that Love of some kind is the only possible explanation of the extraordinary amount of suffering that there is in the world. I cannot conceive any other explanation. I am convinced that there is no other, and that if the worlds have indeed, as I have said, been built out of Sorrow, it has been by the hands of Love, because in no other way could the Soul of man for whom the worlds are made reach the full stature of its perfection. Pleasure for the beautiful body, but Pain for the beautiful Soul.

When I say that I am convinced of these things I speak with too much pride. Far off, like a perfect pearl, one can see the city of God. It is so wonderful that it seems as if a child could reach it in a summer's day. And so a child could. But with me and such as I am it is different. One can realise a thing in a single moment, but one loses it in the long hours that follow with leaden feet. It is so difficult to keep 'heights that the soul is competent to gain.' We think in Eternity, but we move slowly through Time: and how slowly time goes with us who lie in prison I need not speak again, nor of the weariness and despair that creep back into one's cell, and into the cell of one's heart, with such strange insistence that one has as it were to garnish and sweep one's

house for their coming, as for an unwelcome guest, or a bitter master, or a slave whose slave it is one's chance or choice to be. And, though at present you may find it a thing hard to believe, it is true none the less that for you living in freedom and idleness and comfort, it is more easy to learn the lessons of Humility than it is for me, who begin the day by going down on my knees and washing the floor of my cell. For prison-life, with its endless privations and restrictions, makes one rebellious. The most terrible thing about it is not that it breaks one's heart – hearts are made to be broken – but that it turns one's heart to stone. One sometimes feels that it is only with a front of brass and a lip of scorn that one can get through the day at all. And he who is in a state of rebellion cannot receive grace, to use the phrase of which the Church is so fond: so rightly fond I dare say, for in life, as in Art, the mood of rebellion closes up the channels of the soul, and shuts out the airs of heaven. Yet, I must learn these lessons here, if I am to learn them anywhere, and must be filled with joy if my feet are on the right road, and my face set towards 'the gate which is called Beautiful' though I may fall many times in the mire, and often in the mist go astray.

This new life, as through my love of Dante I like sometimes to call it, is, of course, no new life at all, but simply the continuance, by means of development, and Evolution, of my former life. I remember when I was at Oxford saying

to one of my friends – as we were strolling round Magdalen's narrow birdhaunted walks one morning in the June before I took my degree – that I wanted to eat of the fruit of all the trees in the garden of the world, and that I was going out into the world with that passion in my soul. And so, indeed, I went out, and so I lived. My only mistake was that I confined myself so exclusively to the trees of what seemed to me the sun-gilt side of the garden, and shunned the other side for its shadow and its gloom. Failure, disgrace, poverty, sorrow, despair, suffering, tears even, the broken words that come from the lips of pain, remorse that makes one walk in thorns, conscience that condemns, self-abasement that punishes, the misery that puts ashes on its head, the anguish that chooses sackcloth for its raiment and into its own drink puts gall; – all these were things of which I was afraid. And as I had determined to know nothing of them, I was forced to taste each of them in turn, to feed on them, to have for a season, indeed, no other food at all. I don't regret for a single moment having lived for pleasure. I did it to the full, as one should do everything that one does to the full. There was no pleasure I did not experience. I threw the pearl of my soul into a cup of wine. I went down the primrose path to the sound of flutes. I lived on honeycomb. But to have continued the same life would have been wrong because it would have been limiting. I had to pass on. The other half of the garden had its secrets for me also.

De Profundis

Of course all this is foreshadowed and prefigured in my art. Some of it is in *The Happy Prince*, some of it in *The Young King*, notably in the passage where the Bishop says to the kneeling boy, 'Is not He who made misery wiser than thou art'? a phrase which when I wrote it seemed to me little more than a phrase: a great deal of it is hidden away in the note of Doom that like a purple thread runs through the goldcloth of *Dorian Gray*: in *The Critic as Artist* it is set forth in many colours: in *The Soul of Man* it is written down simply and in letters too easy to read: it is one of the refrains whose recurring *motifs* make *Salome* so like a piece of music and bind it together as a ballad: in the prose-poem of the man who from the bronze of the image of the 'Pleasure that liveth for a Moment' has to make the image of the 'Sorrow that abideth for Ever' it is incarnate. It could not have been otherwise. At every single moment of one's life one is what one is going to be no less than what one has been. Art is a symbol, because man is a symbol.

It is, if I can fully attain to it, the ultimate realisation of the artistic life. For the artistic life is simply self-development. Humility in the artist is his frank acceptance of all experiences, just as Love in the artist is simply that sense of Beauty that reveals to the world its body and its soul. In *Marius the Epicurean* Pater seeks to reconcile the artistic life with the life of religion, in the deep, sweet and austere sense of the word. But Marius is little more than a spectator:

an ideal spectator indeed, and one to whom it is given 'to contemplate the spectacle of life with appropriate emotions,' which Wordsworth defines as the poet's true aim: yet a spectator merely, and perhaps a little too much occupied with the comeliness of the vessels of the Sanctuary to notice that it is the Sanctuary of Sorrow that he is gazing at. I see a far more intimate and immediate connection between the true life of Christ and the true life of the artist, and I take a keen pleasure in the reflection that long before Sorrow had made my days her own and bound me to her wheel I had written in *The Soul of Man* that he who would lead a Christ-like life must be entirely and absolutely himself and had taken as my types not merely the shepherd on the hillside and the prisoner in his cell but also the painter to whom the world is a pageant and the poet for whom the world is a song. I remember saying once to André Gide, as we sat together in some Paris *café*, that while metaphysics had but little real interest for me, and Morality absolutely none, there was nothing that either Plato or Christ had said that could not be transferred immediately into the sphere of Art and there find its complete fulfilment. It was a generalisation as profound as it was novel. Nor is it merely that we can discern in Christ that close union of personality with perfection which forms the real distinction between classical and romantic Art and makes Christ the true precursor of the romantic movement in life, but the very

basis of his nature was the same as that of the nature of the artist, an intense and flamelike imagination. He realised in the entire sphere of human relations that imaginative sympathy which in the sphere of Art is the sole secret of creation. He understood the leprosy of the leper, the darkness of the blind, the fierce misery of those who live for pleasure, the strange poverty of the rich. You can see now – can you not? – that when you wrote to me in my trouble, 'When you are not on your pedestal you are not interesting. The next time you are ill I will go away at once,' you were as remote from the true temper of the artist, as you were from what Matthew Arnold calls 'the secret of Jesus'. Either would have taught you that whatever happens to another happens to oneself, and if you want an inscription to read at dawn and at night-time and for pleasure or for pain, write up on the wall of your house in letters for the sun to gild and the moon to silver *'Whatever happens to another happens to oneself,'* and should anyone ask you what such an inscription can possibly mean you can answer that it means 'Lord Christ's heart and Shakespeare's brain'.

Christ's place indeed is with the poets. His whole conception of Humanity sprang right out of the imagination and can only be realised by it. What God was to the Pantheist, man was to Him. He was the first to conceive the divided races as a unity. Before his time there had been gods and men, and, feeling through the mysticism of sympathy that

in himself each had been made incarnate, he calls himself the Son of the One or the son of the other, according to his mood. More than anyone else in history he wakes in us that temper of wonder to which Romance always appeals. There is still something to me almost incredible in the idea of a young Galilean peasant imagining that he could bear on his own shoulders the burden of the entire world: all that had been already done and suffered, and all that was yet to be done and suffered: the sins of Nero, of Caesar Borgia, of Alexander VI., and of him who was Emperor of Rome and Priest of the Sun: the sufferings of those whose name is Legion and whose dwelling is among the tombs, oppressed nationalities, factory children, thieves, people in prison, outcasts, those who are dumb under oppression and whose silence is heard only of God: and not merely imagining this but actually achieving it, so that at the present moment all who come in contact with his personality, even though they may neither bow to his altar nor kneel before his priest, yet somehow find that the ugliness of their sin is taken away and the beauty of their sorrow revealed to them.

I have said of him that he ranks with the poets. That is true. Shelley and Sophocles are of his company. But his entire life also is the most wonderful of poems. For 'pity and terror' there is nothing in the entire cycle of Greek Tragedy to touch it. The absolute purity of the protagonist raises the entire scheme to a height of romantic art from

which the sufferings of 'Thebes and Pelops line' are by their very horror excluded, and shows how wrong Aristotle was when he said in his treatise on the Drama that it would be impossible to bear the spectacle of one blameless in pain: nor in Æschylus or Dante, those stern masters of tenderness, in Shakespeare, the most purely human of all the great artists, in the whole of Celtic myth and legend where the loveliness of the world is shown through a mist of tears, and the life of a man is no more than the life of a flower, is there anything that, for sheer simplicity of pathos wedded and made one with sublimity of tragic effect can be said to equal or approach even the last act of Christ's Passion. The little supper with his companions, one of whom had already sold him for a price: the anguish in the quiet moonlit garden: the false friend coming close to him so as to betray him with a kiss: the friend who still believed in him and on whom as on a rock he had hoped to build a House of Refuge for Man, denying him as the bird cried to the dawn; his own utter loneliness, his submission, his acceptance of everything: and along with it all such scenes as the highpriest of Orthodoxy rending his raiment in wrath, and the Magistrate of Civil Justice calling for water in the vain hope of cleansing himself of that stain of innocent blood that makes him the scarlet figure of history: the coronation-ceremony of Sorrow, one of the most wonderful things in the whole of recorded time: the crucifixion of the Innocent One before the eyes of his

mother and of the disciple whom he loved: the soldiers gambling and throwing dice for his clothes; the terrible death by which he gave the world its most eternal symbol, and his final burial in the tomb of the rich man, his body swathed in Egyptian linen with costly spices and perfumes as though he had been a King's son: – when one contemplates all this from the point of view of Art alone one cannot but be grateful that the supreme office of the Church should be the playing of the tragedy without the shedding of blood, the mystical presentation by means of dialogue and costume and gesture even, of the Passion of her Lord, and it is always a source of pleasure and awe to me to remember that the ultimate survival of the Greek chorus, lost elsewhere to art, is to be found in the servitor answering the priest at Mass.

Yet the whole life of Christ – so entirely may Sorrow and Beauty be made one in their meaning and manifestation – is really an idyll, though it ends with the veil of the temple being rent, and the darkness coming over the face of the earth, and the stone rolled to the door of the sepulchre. One always thinks of him as a young bridegroom with his companions, as indeed he somewhere describes himself, or as a shepherd straying through a valley with his sheep in search of green meadow or cool stream, or as a singer trying to build out of the music the walls of the City of God, or as a lover for whose love the whole world was too small. His miracles seem to me to be as exquisite as the coming of Spring, and quite as natural.

I see no difficulty at all in believing that such was the charm of his personality that his mere presence could bring peace to souls in anguish, and that those who touched his garments or his hands forgot their pain: or that as he passed by on the highway of life people who had seen nothing of life's mysteries, saw them clearly, and others who had been deaf to every voice but that of Pleasure heard for the first time the voice of Love and found it as 'musical as is Apollo's lute': or that evil passions fled at his approach, and men whose dull unimaginative lives had been but a mode of death rose as it were from the grave when he called them: or that when he taught on the hillside the multitude forgot their hunger and thirst and the cares of this world, and that to his friends who listened to him as he sat at meat the coarse food seemed delicate, and the water had the taste of good wine, and the whole house became full of the odour and sweetness of nard. Renan in his *Vie de Jésus* – that gracious Fifth Gospel, the Gospel according to St. Thomas one might call it – says somewhere that Christ's great achievement was that he made himself as much loved after his death as he had been during his lifetime. And certainly, if his place is among the poets, he is the leader of all the lovers. He saw that love was the lost secret of the world for which the wise men had been looking, and that it was only through love that one could approach either the heart of the leper or the feet of God. And above all, Christ is the most supreme of Individualists. Humility, like the artistic

acceptance of all experiences, is merely a mode of manifestation. It is man's soul that Christ is always looking for. He
calls it 'God's Kingdom' – ἡ Βασιλεία τον θιου – and finds
it in every one. He compares it to little things, to a tiny seed,
to a handful of leaven, to a pearl. That is because one only
realises one's soul by getting rid of all alien passions, all acquired
culture, and all external possessions be they good or evil. I
bore up against everything with some stubbornness of will
and much rebellion of nature, till I had absolutely nothing
left in the world but Cyril. I had lost my name, my position,
my happiness, my freedom, my wealth. I was a prisoner and
a pauper. But I had still one beautiful thing left, my own
eldest son. Suddenly he was taken away from me by the law.
It was a blow so appalling that I did not know what to do,
so I flung myself on my knees, and bowed my head, and wept
and said, 'The body of a child is as the body of the Lord: I
am not worthy of either.' That moment seemed to save me.
I saw then that the only thing for me was to accept everything.
Since then – curious as it will no doubt sound to you – I
have been happier.

It was of course my soul in its ultimate essence that I
had reached. In many ways I had been its enemy, but I found
it waiting for me as a friend. When one comes in contact
with the soul it makes one simple as a child, as Christ said
one should be. It is tragic how few people ever 'possess their
souls' before they die. 'Nothing is more rare in any man,'

De Profundis

says Emerson, 'than an act of his own.' It is quite true. Most people are other people. Their thoughts are some one else's opinions, their life a mimicry, their passions a quotation. Christ was not merely the supreme Individualist, but he was the first in History. People have tried to make him out an ordinary Philanthropist, like the dreadful philanthropists of the nineteenth century, or ranked him as an Altruist with the unscientific and sentimental. But he was really neither one nor the other. Pity he has, of course, for the poor, for those who are shut up in prisons, for the lowly, for the wretched; but he has far more pity for the rich, for the hard Hedonists, for those who waste their freedom in becoming slaves to things, for those who wear soft raiment and live in Kings' houses. Riches and Pleasure seemed to him to be really greater tragedies than Poverty or Sorrow. And as for Altruism, who knew better than he that it is vocation not volition that determines us, and that one cannot gather grapes of thorns or figs from thistles? To live for others as a definite self-conscious aim was not his creed. It was not the basis of his creed. When he says 'Forgive your enemies', it is not for the sake of the enemy, but for one's own sake that he says so, and because Love is more beautiful than Hate. In his entreaty to the young man who when he looked on he loved, 'Sell all that thou hast and give it to the poor,' it is not of the state of the poor that he is thinking but of the soul of the young man, the lovely soul that wealth was

marring. In his view of life he is one with the artist who knows that by the inevitable law of self-perfection the poet must sing and the sculptor think in bronze and the painter make the world a mirror for his moods, as surely and as certainly as the hawthorn must blossom in Spring and the corn turn to gold at harvest-time and the Moon in her ordered wanderings change from shield to sickle and from sickle to shield. But while Christ did not say to men 'Live for others', he pointed out that there was no difference at all between the lives of others and one's own life. By this means he gave to man an extended, a Titan personality. Since his coming the history of each separate individual is, or can be made, the history of the world. Of course Culture has intensified the personality of man. Art has made us myriad-minded. Those who have the artistic temperament go into exile with Dante and learn how salt is the bread of others, and how steep their stairs: they catch for a moment the serenity and calm of Goethe, and yet know but too well why Baudelaire cried to God –

'O Seigneur donnez moi la force et le courage
De contempler mon corps et mon coeur sans
degout.'

Out of Shakespeare's sonnets they draw, to their own hurt it may be, the secret of his love and make it their own: they

look with new eyes on modern life because they have listened to one of Chopin's nocturnes, or handled Greek things, or read the story of the passion of some dead man for some dead woman whose hair was like threads of fine gold and whose mouth was as a pomegranate. But the sympathy of the artistic temperament is necessarily with what has found expression. In words or in colours, in music or in marble, behind the painted masks of an Æschylean play, or through some Sicilian shepherds' pierced and jointed reeds, the man and his message must have been revealed. To the artist, expression is the only mode under which he can conceive life at all. To him what is dumb is dead. But to Christ it was not so. With a width and wonder of imagination, that fills one almost with awe, he took the entire world of the inarticulate, the voiceless world of pain, as his kingdom, and made of himself its eternal mouthpiece. Those of whom I have spoken, who are dumb under oppression, and 'whose silence is heard only of God,' he chose as his brothers. He sought to become eyes to the blind, ears to the deaf, and a cry in the lips of those whose tongues had been tied. His desire was to be to the myriads who had found no utterance a very trumpet through which they might call to Heaven. And feeling, with the artistic nature of one to whom Sorrow and Suffering were modes through which he could realise his conception of the Beautiful, that an idea is of no value till it becomes incarnate and is made an image, he makes

of himself the image of the Man of Sorrows, and as such has fascinated and dominated Art as no Greek God ever succeeded in doing. For the Greek Gods in spite of the white and red of their fair fleet limbs were not really what they appeared to be. The curved brow of Apollo was like the sun's disk crescent over a hill at dawn, and his feet were as the wings of the morning, but he himself had been cruel to Marsyas and had made Niobe childless: in the steel shields of the eyes of Pallas there had been no pity for Arachne: the pomp and peacocks of Hera were all that was really noble about her: and the Father of the Gods himself had been too fond of the daughters of men. The two deep suggestive figures of Greek mythology were, for religion, Demeter, an Earth-Goddess, not one of the Olympians, and, for art, Dionysus, the son of a mortal woman to whom the moment of his birth had proved the moment of her death also. But Life itself from its lowliest and most humble sphere produced one far more marvellous than the mother of Proserpina or the son of Semele. Out of the carpenter's shop at Nazareth had come a personality infinitely greater than any made by myth or legend, and one, strangely enough, destined to reveal to the world the mystical meaning of wine and the real beauty of the lilies of the field as none, either on Cithaeron or at Enna, had ever done it. The song of Isaiah: *'He is despised and rejected of men, a man of sorrows and acquainted with grief: and we hid as it were our faces from*

him,' had seemed to him to be prefiguring of himself, and in him the prophecy was fulfilled. We must not be afraid of such a phrase. Every single work of art is the fulfilment of a prophecy. For every work of art is the conversion of an idea into an image. Every single human being should be the fulfilment of a prophecy. For every human being should be the realisation of some ideal either in the mind of God or in the mind of man. Christ found the type, and fixed it, and the dream of a Virgilian poet, either at Jerusalem or at Babylon, became in the long progress of the centuries incarnate in him for whom the world was waiting. *'His visage was marred more than any man's, and his form more than the sons of men'*, are among the signs noted by Isaiah as distinguishing the new ideal, and as soon as Art understood what was meant it opened like a flower at the presence of one in whom truth in Art was set forth as it had never been before. For is not truth in Art, as I have said, 'that in which the outward is expressive of the inward; in which the soul is made flesh, and the body instinct with spirit; in which Form reveals'? To me one of the things in history the most to be regretted is that the Christ's own Renaissance which had produced the cathedral of Chartres, the Arthurian cycle of legends, the life of St. Francis of Assisi, the art of Giotto, and Dante's *Divine Comedy*, was not allowed to develop on its own lines but was interrupted and spoiled by the dreary classical Renaissance that gave us Petrarch, and Raphael's

frescoes, and Palladian architecture, and formal French tragedy, and St. Paul's Cathedral, and Pope's poetry, and every thing that is made from without and by dead rules, and does not spring from within through some spirit informing it. But wherever there is a romantic movement in Art, there somehow, and under some form, is Christ, or the soul of Christ. He is in *Romeo and Juliet*, in *The Winter's Tale*, in Provençal poetry, in the *Ancient Mariner*, in *La Belle Dame sans Merci*, and in Chatterton's *Ballad of Charity*. We owe to him the most diverse things and people. Hugo's *Les Misérables*, Baudelaire's *Fleurs du Mal*, the note of pity in Russian novels, the stained glass and tapestries and quattro-cento work of Burne-Jones and Morris, Verlaine and Verlaine's poems, belong to him no less than the tower of Giotto, Lancelot and Guinevere, Tannhäuser, the troubled romantic marbles of Michael Angelo, pointed architecture, and the love of children and flowers – for both of whom, indeed, in classical art there was but little place, hardly enough for them to grow or play in, but who, from the twelfth century down to our own day have been continually making their appearance in art, under various modes and at various times, coming fitfully and wilfully as children and flowers are apt to do, Spring always seeming to one as if the flowers had been hiding, and only came out into the sun because they were afraid that grown-up people would grow tired of looking for them and give up the search, and

the life of a child being no more than an April day on which there is both rain and sun for the narcissus. And it is the imaginative quality of Christ's own nature that makes him this palpitating centre of romance. The strange figures of poetic drama and ballad are made by the imagination of others, but out of his own imagination entirely did Jesus of Nazareth create himself. The cry of Isaiah had really no more to do with his coming, than the song of the nightingale has to do with the rising of the moon, – no more, though perhaps no less. He was the denial as well as the affirmation of prophecy. For every expectation that he fulfilled, there was another that he destroyed. 'In all beauty,' says Bacon, 'there is some strangeness of proportion,' and of those who are born of the spirit, of those, that is to say, who like himself are dynamic forces, Christ says that they are like the wind that 'bloweth where it listeth, and no man can tell whence it cometh and whither it goeth.' That is why he is so fascinating to artists. He has all the colour-elements of life: mystery, strangeness, pathos, suggestion, ecstasy, love. He appeals to the temper of wonder, and creates that mood by which alone he can be understood. And it is to me a joy to remember that if he is 'of imagination all compact', the world itself is of the same substance. I said in *Dorian Gray* that the great sins of the world take place in the brain, but it is in the brain that everything takes place. We know now that we do not see with the eye or hear with the ear.

They are merely channels for the transmission, adequate or inadequate, of sense-impressions. It is in the brain that the poppy is red, that the apple is odorous, that the skylark sings.

Of late I have been studying the four prose-poems about Christ with some diligence. At Christmas I managed to get hold of a Greek Testament, and every morning, after I have cleaned my cell and polished my tins, I read a little of the Gospels, a dozen verses taken by chance anywhere. It is a delightful way of opening the day. To you, in your turbulent, ill-disciplined life, it would be a capital thing if you would do the same. It would do you no end of good, and the Greek is quite simple. Endless repetition, in and out of season, has spoiled for us the *naïveté*, the freshness, the simple romantic charm of the Gospels. We hear them read far too often, and far too badly, and all repetition is anti-spiritual. When one returns to the Greek; it is like going into a garden of lilies out of some narrow and dark house. And to me the pleasure is doubled by the reflection that it is extremely probable that we have the actual terms, the ipsissima verba, used by Christ. It was always supposed that Christ talked in Aramaic. Even Renan thought so. But now we know that the Galilean peasants, like the Irish peasants of our own day, were bilingual, and that Greek was the ordinary language of intercourse all over Palestine, as indeed all over the Eastern world. I never liked the idea that we knew of Christ's own words only through a translation of a translation. It is a delight to

me to think that as far as his conversation was concerned, Charmides might have listened to him, and Socrates reasoned with him, and Plato understood him: that he really said Εγώ ειμι ό ποιμήν ό καλος, that when he thought of the lilies of the field and how they neither toil nor spin, his absolute expression was, Καταμαθετε τα κρίνα του αγρου τως αυξανει: ου κοπια, ουδε νηθει, and that his last word when he cried out 'my life has been completed, has reached its fulfilment, has been perfected,' was exactly as St. John tells us it was: Τετέλεσται: no more. And while in reading the Gospels – particularly that of St. John himself, or whatever early Gnostic took his name and mantle – I see the continual assertion of the imagination as the basis of all spiritual and material life, I see also that to Christ imagination was simply a form of Love, and that to him Love was Lord in the fullest meaning of the phrase. Some six weeks ago I was allowed by the Doctor to have white bread to eat instead of the coarse black or brown bread of ordinary prison fare. It is a great delicacy. To you it will sound strange that dry bread could possibly be a delicacy to anyone. I assure you that to me it is so much so that at the close of each meal I carefully eat whatever crumbs may be left on my tin plate, or have fallen on the rough towel that one uses as a cloth so as not to soil one's table: and do so, not from hunger – I get now quite sufficient food – but simply in order that nothing should be wasted of what is given to me.

So one should look on love. Christ, like all fascinating personalities, had the power of not merely saying beautiful things himself, but of making other people say beautiful things to him; and I love the story St. Mark tells us about the Greek woman – the γυνή Ελληνις – who, when as a trial of her faith he said to her that he could not give her the bread of the children of Israel, answered him that the little dogs – κυναρια, 'little dogs' it should be rendered – who are under the table eat of the crumbs that the children let fall. Most people live *for* love and admiration. But it is *by* love and admiration that we should live. If any love is shown us we should recognise that we are quite unworthy of it. Nobody is worthy to be loved. The fact that God loves man shows us that in the divine order of ideal things it is written that eternal love is to be given to what is eternally unworthy. Or if that phrase seems to be a bitter one to hear, let us say that everyone is worthy of love, except he who thinks that he is. Love is a sacrament that should be taken kneeling, and *Domine, non sum dignus* should be on the lips and in the hearts of those who receive it. I wish you would sometimes think of that. You need it so much.

If I ever write again, in the sense of producing artistic work, there are just two subjects on which and through which I desire to express myself: one is 'Christ, as the precursor of the romantic movement in life': the other is 'the artistic life considered in its relation to Conduct.' The first is, of course, intensely fascinating, for I see in Christ not merely the essentials of the supreme romantic type, but all the accidents, the wilfulnesses even, of the romantic temperament also. He was the first person who ever said to people that they should live 'flower-like' lives. He fixed the phrase. He took children as the type of what people should try to become. He held them up as examples to their elders, which I myself have always thought the chief use of children, if what is perfect should have a use. Dante describes the soul of a man as coming from the hand of God 'weeping and laughing like a little child,' and Christ also saw that the soul of each one should be *a guisa di fanciulla che piangendo e ridendo pargoleggia*. He felt that life was changeful, fluid, active, and that to allow it to be stereotyped into any form was death. He saw that people should not be too serious over material, common interests: that to be unpractical was a great thing: that one should not bother too much over affairs. The birds didn't, why should man? He is charming when he says, 'Take no thought for the morrow. Is not the *soul* more than meat? Is not the *body* more than raiment?' A Greek might have said the latter phrase. It is full of Greek feeling. But only Christ could have said both, and so summed up life perfectly for us. His morality is all sympathy, just what morality should be. If the only thing that he had ever said had been 'Her sins are forgiven her because she loved much,' it would have been worth while dying to have said

it. His justice is all poetical justice, exactly what justice should be. The beggar goes to heaven because he had been unhappy. I can't conceive a better reason for his being sent there. The people who work for an hour in the vineyard in the cool of the evening receive just as much reward as those who had toiled there all day long in the hot sun. Why shouldn't they? Probably no one deserved anything. Or perhaps they were a different kind of people. Christ had no patience with the dull lifeless mechanical systems that treat people as if they were things, and so treat everybody alike: for him there were no laws: there were exceptions merely, as if anybody, or anything, for that matter, was like aught else in the world. That which is the very keynote of romantic art was to him the proper basis of actual life. He saw no other basis. And when they brought him one taken in the very act of sin and showed him her sentence written in the law and asked him what was to be done, he wrote with his finger on the ground as though he did not hear them, and finally, when they pressed him again and again, looked up and said 'Let him of you who has never sinned be the first to throw the stone at her.' It was worth while living to have said that. Like all poetical natures, he loved ignorant people. He knew that in the soul of one who is ignorant there is always room for a great idea. But he could not stand stupid people, especially those who are made stupid by education, people who are full of opinions not one of which they even understand, a

peculiarly modern type, and one summed up by Christ when he describes it as the type of one who has the key of knowledge, can't use it himself, and won't allow other people to use it, though it may be made to open the gate of God's Kingdom. His chief war was against the Philistines. That is the war every child of light has to wage. Philistinism was the note of the age and community in which he lived. In their heavy inaccessibility to ideas, their dull respectability, their tedious orthodoxy, their worship of vulgar success, their entire preoccupation with the gross materialistic side of life, and their ridiculous estimate of themselves and their importance, the Jews of Jerusalem in Christ's day were the exact counterpart of the British Philistine of our own. Christ mocked at the 'whited sepulchre' of respectability, and fixed that phrase for ever. He treated worldly success as a thing absolutely to be despised. He saw nothing in it at all. He looked on wealth as an incumbrance to a man. He would not hear of life being sacrificed to any system of thought or morals. He pointed out that forms or ceremonies were made for man, not man for forms and ceremonies. He took Sabbatarianism as a type of the things that should be set at nought. The cold philanthropies, the ostentatious public charities, the tedious formalisms so dear to the middle-class mind he exposed with utter and relentless scorn. To us, what is termed Orthodoxy is merely a facile unintelligent acquiescence; but to them, and in their hands, it was a terrible

and paralysing tyranny. Christ swept it aside. He showed that the spirit alone was of value. He took a keen pleasure in pointing out to them that though they were always reading the Law and the Prophets they had not really the smallest idea of what either of them meant. In opposition to their tithing of each separate day into its fixed routine of prescribed duties, as they tithed mint and rue, he preached the enormous importance of living completely for the moment. Those whom he saved from their sins are saved simply for beautiful moments in their lives. Mary Magdalen, when she sees Christ, breaks the rich vase of alabaster that one of her seven lovers had given her and spills the odorous spices over his tired dusty feet, and for that one moment's sake sits for ever with Ruth and Beatrice in the tresses of the snow-white Rose of Paradise. All that Christ says to us by way of a little warning is that *every* moment should be beautiful, that the soul should *always* be ready for the coming of the Bridegroom, *always* waiting for the voice of the Lover. Philistinism being simply that side of man's nature that is not illumined by the imagination, he sees all the lovely influences of life as modes of Light: the imagination itself is the world-light, το φως του κοσμομ: the world is made by it, and yet the world cannot understand it: that is because the imagination is simply a manifestation of Love, and it is love, and the capacity for it, that distinguishes one human being from another. But it is when he deals with the Sinner that he is

most romantic, in the sense of most real. The world had always loved the Saint as being the nearest possible approach to the perfection of God. Christ, through some divine instinct in him, seems to have always loved the sinner as being the nearest possible approach to the perfection of man. His primary desire was not to reform people, any more than his primary desire was to a relieve suffering. To turn an interesting thief into a tedious honest man was not his aim. He would have thought little of the Prisoners' Aid Society and other modern movements of the kind. The conversion of a Publican into a Pharisee would not have seemed to him a great achievement by any means. But in a manner not yet understood of the world he regarded sin and suffering as being in themselves beautiful, holy things, and modes of perfection. It *sounds* a very dangerous idea. It is. All great ideas *are* dangerous. That it was Christ's creed admits of no doubt. That it is the true creed I don't doubt myself. Of course the sinner must repent. But why? Simply because otherwise he would be unable to realise what he had done. The moment of repentance is the moment of initiation. More than that. It is the means by which one alters one's past. The Greeks thought that impossible. They often say in their Gnomic aphorisms 'Even the Gods cannot alter the past'. Christ showed that the commonest sinner could do it. That it was the one thing he could do. Christ, had he been asked, would have said – I feel quite certain about it – that the

moment the prodigal son fell on his knees and wept he really made his having wasted his substance with harlots and then kept swine and hungered for the husks they ate beautiful and holy incidents in his life. It is difficult for most people to grasp the idea. I dare say one has to go to prison to understand it. If so, it may be worth while going to prison. There is something so unique about Christ. Of course, just as there are false dawns before the dawn itself, and winter-days so full of sudden sunlight that they will cheat the wise crocus into squandering its gold before its time, and make some foolish bird call to its mate to build on barren boughs, so there were Christians before Christ. For that we should be grateful. The unfortunate thing is that there have been none since. I make one exception, St. Francis of Assisi. But then God had given him at his birth the soul of a poet, as he himself when quite young had in mystical marriage taken Poverty as his bride; and with the soul of a poet and the body of a beggar he found the way to perfection not difficult. He understood Christ, and so he became like him. We do not require the Liber Conformitatum to teach us that the life of St. Francis was the true *Imitatio Christi*; a poem compared to which the book of that name is merely prose. Indeed, that is the charm about Christ, when all is said. He is just like a work of art. He does not really teach one anything, but by being brought into his presence one becomes something. And everybody is predestined to his presence. Once

at least in his life each man walks with Christ to Emmaus.

As regards the other subject, the relation of the artistic life to conduct, it will no doubt seem strange to you that I should select it. People point to Reading Gaol, and say 'That is where the artistic life leads a man.' Well, it might lead one to worse places. The more mechanical people to whom life is a shrewd speculation dependent on a careful calculation of ways and means, always know where they are going, and go there. They start with the ideal desire of being the Parish Beadle, and, in whatever sphere they are placed, they succeed in being the Parish Beadle and no more. A man whose desire is to be something separate from himself, to be a member of Parliament, or a successful grocer, or a prominent Solicitor, or a judge, or something equally tedious, invariably succeeds in being what he wants to be. That is his punishment. Those who want a mask have to wear it. But with the dynamic forces of life, and those in whom those dynamic forces become incarnate, it is different. People whose desire is solely for self-realisation never know where they are going. They can't know. In one sense of the word it is, of course, necessary, as the Greek oracle said, to know oneself. That is the first achievement of knowledge. But to recognise that the soul of a man is unknowable is the ultimate achievement of Wisdom. The final mystery is oneself. When one has weighed the sun in a balance, and measured the steps of the moon, and mapped out the seven heavens star

by star, there still remains oneself. Who can calculate the orbit of his own soul? When the son of Kish went out to look for his father's asses, he did not know that a man of God was waiting for him with the very chrism of coronation, and that his own soul was already the soul of a King.

I hope to live long enough, and to produce work of such a character, that I shall be able at the end of my days to say, 'Yes: this is just where the artistic life leads a man.' Two of the most perfect lives I have come across in my own experience are the lives of Verlaine and of Prince Kropotkine: both of them men who passed years in prison: the first, the one Christian poet since Dante, the other, a man with a soul of that beautiful white Christ that seems coming out of Russia. And for the last seven or eight months, in spite of a succession of great troubles reaching me from the outside world almost without intermission, I have been placed in direct contact with a new spirit working in this prison through men and things, that has helped me beyond any possibility of expression in words; so that while for the first year of my imprisonment I did nothing else, and can remember doing nothing else, but wring my hands in impotent despair, and say 'What an ending! What an appalling ending!' now I try to say to myself, and sometimes when I am not torturing myself do really and sincerely say, 'What a beginning! What a wonderful beginning!' It may really be so. It may become so. If it does I shall owe much

to this new personality that has altered every man's life in this place. Things in themselves are of little importance, have indeed, – let us for once thank Metaphysics for something that she has taught us – no real existence. The spirit alone is of importance. Punishment may be inflicted in such a way that it will heal, not make a wound, just as alms may be given in such a manner that the bread changes to a stone in the hands of the giver. What a change there is – not in the regulations, for they are fixed by iron rule, but in the spirit that uses them as its expression – you can realise when I tell you that had I been released last May, as I tried to be, I would have left this place, loathing it and every official in it with a bitterness of hatred that would have poisoned my life. I have had a year longer of imprisonment, but Humanity has been in the prison along with us all, and now when I go out I shall always remember great kindnesses that I have received here from almost everybody, and on the day of my release will give my thanks to many people and ask to be remembered by them in turn. The prison system is absolutely and entirely wrong. I would give anything to be able to alter it when I go out. I intend to try. But there is nothing in the world so wrong but that the spirit of Humanity, which is the spirit of Love, the spirit of the Christ who is not in Churches, may make it, if not right, at least possible to be borne without too much bitterness of heart. I know also that much is waiting for me outside, that is very delightful,

from what St. Francis of Assisi calls '*my brother the wind*'
and '*my sister the rain*', lovely things both of them, down to
the shop windows and sunsets of great cities. If I made a
list of all that still remains to me, I don't know where I
should stop: for, indeed, God made the world just as much
for me as for anyone else. Perhaps I may go out with something I had not got before. I need not tell you that to me
Reformations in Morals are as meaningless and vulgar as
Reformations in Theology. But while to propose to be a
better man is a piece of unscientific cant, to have become a
deeper man is the privilege of those who have suffered. And
such I think I have become. You can judge for yourself. If
after I go out a friend of mine gave a feast, and did not
invite me to it, I shouldn't mind a bit. I can be perfectly
happy by myself. With freedom, books, flowers, and the
moon, who could not be happy? Besides, feasts are not for
me any more. I have given too many to care about them.
That side of life is over for me, very fortunately, I dare say.
But if, after I go out, a friend of mine had a sorrow, and
refused to allow me to share it, I should feel it most bitterly.
If he shut the doors of the house of mourning against me
I would come back again and again and beg to be admitted,
so that I might share in what I was entitled to share in. If
he thought me unworthy, unfit to weep with him, I should
feel it as the most poignant humiliation, as the most terrible
mode in which disgrace could be inflicted on me. But that

could not be. I have a right to share in Sorrow, and he who can look at the loveliness of the world, and share its sorrow, and realise something of the wonder of both, is in immediate contact with divine things, and has got as near to God's secret as anyone can get. Perhaps there may come into my art also, no less than into my life, a still deeper note, one of greater unity of passion, and directness of impulse. Not width but intensity is the true aim of modern Art. We are no longer in Art concerned with the type. It is with the exception we have to do. I cannot put my sufferings into any form they took, I need hardly say. Art only begins, where Imitation ends. But something must come into my work, of fuller memory of words perhaps, of richer cadences, of more curious colour-effects, of simpler architectural-order, of some aesthetic quality at any rate. When Marsyas was 'torn from the scabbard of his limbs' – *della vagina della membre sue* – to use one of Dante's most terrible Tacitean phrases – he had no more song, the Greeks said. Apollo had been victor. The lyre had vanquished the reed. But perhaps the Greeks were mistaken. I hear in much modern Art the cry of Marsyas. It is bitter in Baudelaire, sweet and plaintive in Lamartine, mystic in Verlaine. It is in the deferred resolutions of Chopin's music. It is in the discontent that haunts the recurrent faces of Burne-Jones's women. Even Matthew Arnold, whose song of Callicles tells of 'the triumph of the sweet persuasive lyre,' and the 'famous final victory,' in such a clear note of lyrical

beauty – even he, in the hushed undertone of doubt and distress that haunts his verse, has not a little of it; in the troubled undertone of doubt and distress that haunts his verses, neither Goethe nor Wordsworth could heal him, though he followed each in turn, and when he seeks to mourn for *Thyrsis* or to sing of the *Scholar Gipsy*, it is the reed that he has to take for the rendering of his strain. But whether or not the Phrygian Faun was silent, I cannot be. Expression is as necessary to me as leaf and blossom are to the black branches of the trees that show themselves above the prison walls and are so restless in the wind. Between my art and the world there is now a wide gulf, but between art and myself there is none. I hope at least that there is none. To each of us different fates are meted out. Freedom, pleasure, amusements, a life of ease have been your lot, and you are not worthy of it. My lot has been one of public infamy, of long imprisonment, of misery, of ruin, of disgrace, and I am not worthy of it either – not yet, at any rate. I remember that I used to say that I thought I could bear a real tragedy if it came to me with purple pall and a mask of noble sorrow, but that the dreadful thing about modernity was that it put Tragedy into the raiment of Comedy, so that the great realities seemed commonplace or grotesque or lacking in style. It is quite true about modernity. It has probably always been true about actual life. It is said that all martyrdoms seemed mean to the looker-on. The nine-

De Profundis

teenth century is no exception to the general rule. Everything about my tragedy has been hideous, mean, repellent, lacking in style. Our very dress makes us grotesques. We are the zanies of sorrow. We are clowns whose hearts are broken. We are specially designed to appeal to the sense of humour. On November 13th 1895 I was brought down here from London. From two o'clock till half past two on that day I had to stand on the centre platform of Clapham Junction in convict dress and handcuffed, for the world to look at. I had been taken out of the Hospital Ward, without a moment's notice being given to me. Of all possible objects *I* was the most grotesque. When people saw me they laughed. Each train as it came up swelled the audience. Nothing could exceed their amusement. That was, of course before they knew who I was. As soon as they had been informed, they laughed still more. For half an hour I stood there in the grey November rain surrounded by a jeering mob. For a year after that was done to me I wept every day at the same hour and for the same space of time. That is not such a tragic thing as possibly it sounds to you. To those who are in prison, tears are a part of every day's experience. A day in prison on which one does not weep is a day on which one's heart is hard, not a day on which one's heart is happy.

Well, now I am really beginning to feel more regret for the people who laughed, than for myself. Of course when they saw me I was not on my pedestal, I was in the pillory.

But it is a very unimaginative nature that only cares for people on their pedestals. A pedestal may be a very unreal thing. A pillory is a terrific reality. They should have known also how to interpret sorrow better. I have said that behind sorrow there is always sorrow. It were still wiser to say that behind sorrow there is always a soul. And to mock at a soul in pain is a dreadful thing. Unbeautiful are their lives who do it. In the strangely simple economy of the world people only get what they give, and to those who have not enough imagination to penetrate the mere outward of things, and feel pity, what pity can be given save that of scorn? I have told you this account of the mode of my being conveyed here simply that you should realise how hard it has been for me to get anything out of my punishment but bitterness and despair. I have however to do it, and now and then I have moments of submission and acceptance. All the spring may be hidden in the single bud, and the low ground-nest of the lark may hold the joy that is to herald the feet of many rose-red dawns, and so perhaps whatever beauty of life still remains to me is contained in some moment of surrender, abasement and humiliation. I can, at any rate, merely proceed on the lines of my own development, and by accepting all that has happened to me make myself worthy of it. People used to say of me that I was too individualistic. I must be far more of an individualist than I ever was. I must get far more out of myself than I ever got, and ask far

less of the world than I ever asked. Indeed my ruin came, not from too great individualism of life, but from too little. The one disgraceful, unpardonable, and to all time contemptible action of my life was my allowing myself to be forced into appealing to Society for help and protection against your Father. To have made such an appeal against anyone would have been from the individualist point of view bad enough, but what excuse can there ever be put forward for having made it against one of such nature and aspect? ... Of course once I had put into motion the forces of Society, Society turned on me and said, 'Have you been living all this time in defiance of my laws, and do you now appeal to those laws for protection? You shall have those laws exercised to the full. You shall abide by what you have appealed to.' The result is I am in gaol. And I used to feel bitterly the irony and ignominy of my position when in the course of my three trials, beginning at the Police Court, I used to see your Father bustling in and out in the hopes of attracting public attention, as if anyone could fail to note or remember the stableman's gait and dress, the bowed legs, the twitching hands, the hanging lower lip, the bestial and half-witted grin. Even when he was not there, or was out of sight, I used to feel conscious of his presence, and the blank dreary walls of the great Court-room, the very air itself, seemed to me at times to be hung with multitudinous masks of that apelike face. Certainly no man ever fell so ignobly, and by

such ignoble instruments, as I did. I say, in *Dorian Gray* somewhere, that 'a man cannot be too careful in the choice of his enemies.' I little thought that it was by a pariah that I was to be made a pariah myself.

This urging me, forcing me to appeal to Society for help, is one of the things that make me despise you so much, that make me despise myself so much for having yielded to you. Your not appreciating me as an artist was quite excusable. It was temperamental. You couldn't help it. But you might have appreciated me as an Individualist. For that no culture was required. But you didn't, and so you brought the element of Philistinism into a life that had been a complete protest against it, and from some points of view a complete annihilation of it. The Philistine element in life is not the failure to understand Art. Charming people such as fishermen, shepherds, ploughboys, peasants and the like, know nothing about Art, and are the very salt of the Earth. He is the Philistine who upholds and aids the heavy, cumbrous, blind, mechanical forces of Society, and who does not recognise dynamic force when he meets it either in a man or a movement.

People thought it dreadful of me to have entertained at dinner the Evil things of life, and to have found pleasure in their company. But they, from the point of view through which I, as an artist in life, approached them were delightfully suggestive and stimulating. The danger was half the

excitement. It was like feasting with panthers. I used to feel as the snake-charmer must feel when he lures the cobra to stir from the painted cloth or reed-basket that holds it, and makes it spread its hood at his bidding, and sway to and fro in the air as a plant sways restfully in a stream. They were to me the brightest of gilded snakes. Their poison was part of their perfection, I did not know that when they were to strike at me it was to be at your piping and for your father's pay. I don't feel at all ashamed of having known them. They were intensely interesting. What I do feel ashamed of is the horrible Philistine atmosphere into which you brought me. My business as an artist was with Ariel. You set me to wrestle with Caliban. Instead of making beautiful coloured, musical things such as *Salome*, and the *Florentine Tragedy*, and *La Sainte Courtisane*, I found myself forced to send long lawyer's letters to your father, and constrained to appeal to the very things against which I had always protested. Clibborn and Atkins were wonderful in their infamous war against life. To entertain them was an astounding adventure. Dumas *père*, Cellini, Goya, Edgar Allan Poe, or Baudelaire, would have done just the same. What is loathsome to me is the memory of interminable visits paid by me to the solicitor Humphreys in your company, when in the ghastly glare of a bleak room you and I would sit with serious faces telling serious lies to a bald man, till I really groaned and yawned with *ennui*. *There* is where I found myself after two years friendship with you,

right in the centre of Philistia, away from everything that was beautiful, or brilliant, or wonderful, or daring. At the end, I had to come forward, on your behalf, as the champion of Respectability in conduct, of Puritanism in life, and of Morality in Art. *Voila ou mènent les mauvais chemins!*

And the curious thing to me is that you should have tried to imitate your Father in his chief characteristics. I cannot understand why he was to you an exemplar, where he should have been a warning, except that whenever there is hatred between two people there is bond or brotherhood of some kind. I suppose that, by some strange law of the antipathy of similars, you loathed each other, not because in so many points you were so different, but because in some you were so like. In June 1893 when you left Oxford, without a degree and with debts, petty in themselves, but considerable to a man of your Father's income, your Father wrote you a very vulgar, violent and abusive letter. The letter you sent him in reply was in every way worse, and of course far less excusable, and consequently you were extremely proud of it. I remember quite well your saying to me with your most conceited air that you could beat your father 'at his own trade'. Quite true. But what a trade! What a competition! You used to laugh and sneer at your Father for retiring from your cousin's house where he was living in order to write filthy letters to him from a neighbouring hotel. You used to do just the same to me. You constantly lunched with me at some public restaurant,

sulked or made a scene during luncheon, and then retired to White's Club and wrote me a letter of the very foulest character. The only difference between you and your father was that after you had despatched your letter to me by special messenger, you would arrive yourself at my rooms some hours later, not to apologise, but to know if I had ordered dinner at the Savoy, and if not, why not. Sometimes you would actually arrive before the offensive letter had been read. I remember on one occasion you had asked me to invite to luncheon at the *Cafe Royal* two of your friends, one of whom I had never seen in my life. I did so, and at your special request ordered beforehand a specially luxurious luncheon to be prepared. The *Chef*, I remember, was sent for, and particular instructions given about the wines. Instead of coming to luncheon you sent me at the *Cafe* an abusive letter, timed so as to reach me after we had been waiting half an hour for you. I read the first line, and saw what it was, and putting the letter in my pocket, explained to your friends that you were suddenly taken ill, and that the rest of the letter referred to your symptoms. In point of fact I did not read the letter till I was dressing for dinner at Tite Street that evening. As I was in the middle of its mire, wondering with infinite sadness how you could write letters that were really like the froth and foam on the lips of an epileptic, my servant came in to tell me that you were in the hall and were very anxious to see me for five minutes. I at once sent down and asked you to

come up. You arrived, looking I admit very frightened and pale, to beg my advice and assistance, as you had been told that a man from Lumley the Solicitor had been enquiring for you at Cadogan Place, and you were afraid that your Oxford trouble or some new danger was threatening you. I consoled you, told you, what proved to be the case, that it was merely a tradesman's bill probably, and let you stay to dinner, and pass your evening with me. You never mentioned a single word about your hideous letter, nor did I. I treated it as simply an unhappy symptom of an unhappy temperament. The subject was never alluded to. To write to me a loathsome letter at 2.30, and fly to me for help and sympathy at 7.15 the same afternoon, was a perfectly ordinary occurrence in your life. You went quite beyond your Father in such habits, as you did in others. When his revolting letters to you were read in open Court he naturally felt ashamed and pretended to weep. Had your letters to him been read by his own Counsel still more horror and repugnance would have been felt by everyone. Nor was it merely in style that you 'beat him at his own trade', but in mode of attack you distanced him completely. You availed yourself of the public telegram, and the open postcard. I think you might have left such modes of annoyance to people like Alfred Wood whose sole source of income it is. Don't you? What was a profession to him and his class was a pleasure to you, and a very evil one. Nor have you given up your horrible habit of writing offensive

letters, after all that has happened to me through them and for them. You still regard it as one of your accomplishments, and you exercise it on my friends, on those who have been kind to me in prison like Robert Sherard and others. That is disgraceful of you. When Robert Sherard heard from me that I did not wish you to publish any article on me in the *Mercure de France*, with or without letters, you should have been grateful to him for having ascertained my wishes on the point, and for having saved you from, without intending it, inflicting more pain on me than you had done already. You must remember that a patronising and Philistine letter about 'fair play' for a 'man who is down' is all right for an English newspaper. It carries on the old traditions of English journalism in regard to their attitude towards artists. But in France such a tone would have exposed me to ridicule and you to contempt. I could not have allowed any article till I had known its aim, temper, mode of approach and the like. In art, good intentions are not of the smallest value. All bad art is the result of good intentions.

Nor is Robert Sherard the only one of my friends to whom you have addressed acrimonious and bitter letters because they sought that my wishes and my feelings should be consulted in matters concerning myself, the publication of articles on me, the dedication of your verses, the surrender of my letters and presents, and such like. You have annoyed or sought to annoy others also.

Does it ever occur to you what an awful position I would have been in if for the last two years, during my appalling sentence, I had been dependent on you as a friend? Do you ever think of that? Do you ever feel any gratitude to those who by kindness without stint, devotion without limit, cheerfulness and joy in giving, have lightened my black burden for me, have visited me again and again, have written to me beautiful and sympathetic letters, have managed my affairs for me, have arranged my future life for me, have stood by me in the teeth of obloquy, taunt, open sneer or insult even? I thank God every day that he gave me friends other than you. I owe everything to them. The very books in my cell are paid for by Robbie out of his pocket-money. From the same source are to come clothes for me, when I am released. I am not ashamed of taking a thing that is given by love and affection. I am proud of it. But do you ever think of what my friends such as More Adey, Robbie, Robert Sherard, Frank Harris, and Arthur Clifton, have been to me in giving me comfort, help, affection, sympathy and the like ? I suppose that has never dawned on you. And yet – if you had any imagination in you – you would know that there is not a single person who has been kind to me in my prison-life, down to the warder who may give me a good-morning or a good-night that is not one of his prescribed – down to the common policemen who in their homely rough way strove to comfort me on my journeys to and fro from the Bankruptcy

Court under conditions of terrible mental distress – down to the poor thief who recognising me as we tramped round the yard at Wandsworth whispered to me in the hoarse prison-voice men get from long and compulsory silence: '*I am sorry for you: it is harder for the likes of you than it is for the likes of us*': – not one of them all, I say, the very mire from whose shoes you should not be proud to be allowed to kneel down and clean.

Have you imagination enough to see what a fearful tragedy it was for me to have come across your family? What a tragedy it would have been for anyone at all, who had a great position, a great name, anything of importance to lose? There is hardly one of the elders of your family – with the exception of Percy, who is really a good fellow – who did not in some way contribute to my ruin....

I have spoken of your mother to you with some bitterness, and I strongly advise you to let her see this letter, for your own sake chiefly. If it is painful to her to read such an indictment against one of her sons, let her remember that *my* mother, who intellectually ranks with Elizabeth Barrett-Browning, and historically with Madame Roland, died brokenhearted because the son of whose genius and art she had been so proud, and whom she had regarded always as a worthy continuer of a distinguished name, had been condemned to the treadmill for two years. You will ask me in what way your mother contributed to my destruction. I

will tell you. Just as you strove to shift on to me all your immoral responsibilities, so your mother strove to shift on to me all her moral responsibilities with regard to you. Instead of speaking directly to you about your life, as a mother should, she always wrote privately to me with earnest, frightened entreaties not to let you know that she was writing to me. You see the position in which I was placed between you and your mother. It was one as false, as absurd, and as tragic as the one in which I was placed between you and your father. In August 1892, and on the 8th of November in the same year I had two long interviews with your mother about you. On both occasions I asked her why she did not speak directly to you herself. On both occasions she gave the same answer: '*I am afraid to: he gets so angry when he is spoken to.*' The first time, I knew you so slightly that I did not understand what she meant. The second time, I knew you so well that I understood perfectly. (During the interval you had had an attack of jaundice and been ordered by the Doctor to go for a week to Bournemouth, and had induced me to accompany you as you hated being alone.) But the first duty of a mother is not to be afraid of speaking seriously to her son. Had your mother spoken seriously to you about the trouble she saw you were in in July 1892 and made you confide in her it would have been much better, and much happier ultimately for both of you. All the underhand and secret communications with me were wrong. What was the use of your mother

sending me endless little notes, marked 'Private' on the envelope, begging me not to ask you so often to dinner, and not to give you any money, each note ending with an earnest postscript '*On no account let Alfred know that I have written to you.*'? What good could come of such a correspondence? Did you ever wait to be asked to dinner? Never. You took all your meals as a matter of course with me. If I remonstrated, you always had one observation: '*If I don't dine with you, where am I to dine? You don't suppose that I am going to dine at home?*' It was unanswerable. And if I absolutely refused to let you dine with me, you always threatened that you would do something foolish, and always did it. What possible result could there be from letters such as your mother used to send me, except that which did occur, a foolish and fatal shifting of the moral responsibility on to my shoulders? Of the various details in which your mother's weakness and lack of courage proved so ruinous to herself, to you, and to me, I don't want to speak any more, but surely, when she heard of your Father coming down to my house to make a loathsome scene and create a public scandal, she might then have seen that a serious crisis was impending, and taken some serious steps to try and avoid it ? But all she could think of doing was to send down plausible George Wyndham with his pliant tongue to propose to me... what? That I should 'gradually drop you'! As if it had been possible for me to gradually drop you! I had tried to end our friendship in every possible way, going

so far as actually to leave England and give a false address abroad in the hopes of breaking at one blow a bond that had become irksome, hateful, and ruinous to me. Do you think that I *could* have 'gradually dropped' you? Do you think that would have satisfied your Father? You know it would not. What your Father wanted, indeed, was not the cessation of our friendship, but a public scandal. That is what he was striving for. His name had not been in the papers for years. He saw the opportunity of appearing before the British public in an entirely new character, that of the affectionate father. His sense of humour was roused. Had I severed my friendship with you it would have been a terrible disappointment to him, and the small notoriety of a second divorce suit, however revolting its details and origin, would have proved but little consolation to him. For what he was aiming at was popularity, and to pose as a champion of purity, as it is termed, is, in the present condition of the British public, the surest mode of becoming for the nonce a heroic figure. Of this public I have said in one of my plays that if it is Caliban for one half of the year, it is Tartuffe for the other, and your Father, in whom both characters may be said to have become incarnate, was in this way marked out as the proper representative of Puritanism in its aggressive and most characteristic form. No gradual dropping of you would have been of any avail, even had it been practicable. Don't you feel now that the only thing for your mother to have done was to have asked me

to come to see her, and had you and your brother present, and said definitely that the friendship must absolutely cease? She would have found in me her warmest seconder, and with Drumlanrig and myself in the room she need not have been afraid of speaking to you. She did not do so. She was afraid of her responsibilities, and tried to shift them on to me. One letter she did certainly write to me. It was a brief one, to ask me not to send the lawyers' letter to your Father warning him to desist. She was quite right. It was ridiculous my consulting lawyers and seeking their protection. But she nullified any effect her letter might have produced by her usual postscript: '*On no account let Alfred know that I have written to you.*' You were entranced at the idea of my sending lawyers' letters to your father, as well as yourself. It was your suggestion. I could not tell you that your mother was strongly against the idea, for she had bound me with the most solemn promises never to tell you about her letters to me, and I foolishly kept my promise to her. Don't you see that it was wrong of her not to speak directly to you? That all the backstairs-interviews with me, and the area-gate correspondence were wrong? Nobody can shift their responsibilities on anyone else. They always return ultimately to the proper owner. Your one idea of life, your one philosophy, if you are to be credited with a philosophy, was that whatever you did was to be paid for by someone else: I don't mean merely in the financial sense – that was simply the practical application of your philosophy

to everyday life – but in the broadest fullest sense of transferred responsibility. You made that your creed. It was very successful as far as it went. You forced me into taking the action because you knew that your father would not attack your life or yourself in any way, and that I would defend both to the utmost, and take on my own shoulders whatever would be thrust on me. You were quite right. Your father and I, each from different motives of course, did exactly as you counted on our doing. But somehow, in spite of everything, you have not really escaped. The 'infant Samuel theory', as for brevity's sake one may term it, is all very well as far as the general world goes. It may be a good deal scorned in London, and a little sneered at in Oxford, but that is merely because there are a few people who know you in each place, and because in each place you left traces of your passage. Outside of a small set in those two cities, the world looks on you as the good young man who was very nearly tempted into wrong-doing by the wicked and immoral artist, but was rescued just in time by his kind and loving father. It sounds all right. And yet, you know you have not escaped. I am not referring to a silly question asked by a silly juryman, which was of course treated with contempt by the Crown and by the Judge. No one cared about that. I am referring perhaps principally to yourself. In your own eyes, and some day you will have to think of your conduct, you are not, cannot be quite satisfied at the way in which things have turned out.

Secretly you must think of yourself with a good deal of shame. A brazen face is a capital thing to show the world, but now and then when you are alone, and have no audience, you have, I suppose, to take the mask off for mere breathing purposes. Else, indeed, you would be stifled.... And in the same manner your mother must at times regret that she tried to shift her grave responsibilities on someone else, who already had enough of a burden to carry. She occupied the position of both parents to you. Did she really fulfil the duties of either? If I bore with your bad temper and your rudeness and your scenes, she might have borne with them too. When last I saw my wife – fourteen months ago now – I told her that she would have to be to Cyril a father as well as a mother. I told her everything about your mother's mode of dealing with you in every detail as I have set it down in this letter, only of course far more fully. I told her the reason of the endless notes with 'Private' on the envelope that used to come to Tite Street from your mother, so constantly that my wife used to laugh and say that we must be collaborating in a society novel or something of that kind. I implored her not to be to Cyril what your mother was to you. I told her that she should bring him up so that if he shed innocent blood he would come and tell her, that she might cleanse his hands for him first, and then teach him how by penance or expiation to cleanse his soul afterwards. I told her that if she was frightened of facing the responsibility of the life of another,

though her own child, she should get a guardian to help her.
That she has, I am glad to say, done. She has chosen Adrian
Hope, a man of high birth and culture and fine character,
her own cousin, whom you met once at Tite Street, and with
him Cyril and Vivian have a good chance of a beautiful
future. Your mother, if she was afraid of talking seriously to
you, should have chosen someone amongst her own relatives
to whom you might have listened. But she should not have
been afraid. She should have had it out with you and faced
it. At any rate, look at the result. Is she satisfied and pleased?

I know she puts the blame on me. I hear of it, not from
people who know you, but from people who do not know
you, and do not desire to know you. I hear of it often. She
talks of the influence of an elder over a younger man, for
instance. It is one of her favourite attitudes towards the
question, and it is always a successful appeal to popular
prejudice and ignorance. I need not ask you what influence
I had over you. You know I had none. It was one of your
frequent boasts that I had none, and the only one indeed
that was well-founded. What was there, as a mere matter of
fact, in you that I could influence? Your brain? It was
undeveloped. Your imagination? It was dead. Your heart? It
was not yet born. Of all the people who have ever crossed
my life you were the one, and the only one, I was unable in
any way to influence in any direction. When I lay ill and
helpless in a fever caught from tending on you, I had not

sufficient influence over you to induce you to get me even a cup of milk to drink, or to see that I had the ordinary necessaries of a sickroom, or to take the trouble to drive a couple of hundred yards to a booksellers to get me a book at my own expense. When I was actually engaged in writing, and penning comedies that were to beat Congreve for brilliancy, and Dumas *fils* for philosophy, and I suppose everybody else for every other quality, I had not sufficient influence with you to get you to leave me undisturbed as an artist should be left. Wherever my writing room was, it was to you an ordinary lounge, a place to smoke and drink hock-and-seltzer in, and chatter about absurdities. The 'influence of an elder over a younger man' is an excellent theory till it comes to my ears. Then it becomes grotesque. When it comes to your ears, I suppose you smile – to yourself. You are certainly entitled to do so. I hear also much of what she says about money. She states, and with perfect justice, that she was ceaseless in her entreaties to me not to supply you with money. I admit it. Her letters were endless, and the postscript *'Pray do not let Alfred know that I have written to you'* appears in them all. But it was no pleasure to me to have to pay every single thing for you from your morning-shave to your midnight hansom. It was a horrible bore. I used to complain to you again and again about It. I used to tell you – you remember, don't you? – how I loathed your regarding me as a 'useful' person, how no artist wishes to be so regarded or

so treated; artists, like art itself, being of their very essence quite useless. You used to get very angry when I said it to you. The truth always made you angry. Truth, indeed, is a thing that is most painful to listen to and most painful to utter. But it did not make you alter your views or your mode of life. Every day I had to pay for every single thing you did all day long. Only a person of absurd good nature or of indescribable folly would have done so. I unfortunately was a complete combination of both. When I used to suggest that your mother should supply you with the money you wanted, you always had a very pretty and graceful answer. You said that the income allowed her by your father – some £1500 a year I believe – was quite inadequate to the wants of a lady of her position, and that you could not go to her for more money than you were getting already. You were quite right about her income being one absolutely unsuitable to a lady of her position and tastes, but you should not have made that an excuse for living in luxury on me: it should on the contrary have been a suggestion to you for economy in your own life. The fact is that you were, and are I suppose still, a typical sentimentalist. For a sentimentalist is simply one who desires to have the luxury of an emotion without paying for it. To propose to spare your mother's pocket was beautiful. To do so at my expense was ugly. You think that one can have one's emotions for nothing. One cannot. Even the finest and the most self-sacrificing emotions have to be

paid for. Strangely enough, that is what makes them fine. The intellectual and emotional life of ordinary people is a very contemptible affair. Just as they borrow their ideas from a sort of circulating library of thought – the *Zeitgeist* of an age that has no soul – and send them back soiled at the end of each week, so they always try to get their emotions on credit, and refuse to pay the bill when it comes in. You should pass out of that conception of life. As soon as you have to pay for an emotion you will know its quality, and be the better for such knowledge. And remember that the sentimentalist is always a cynic at heart. Indeed sentimentality is merely the bank-holiday of cynicism. And delightful as cynicism is from its intellectual side, now that it has left the Tub for the Club, it never can be more than the perfect philosophy for a man who has no soul. It has its social value, and to an artist all modes of expression are interesting, but in itself it is a poor affair, for to the true cyme nothing is ever revealed. I think that if you look back now to your attitude towards your mother's income, and your attitude towards my income, you will not feel proud of yourself, and perhaps you may someday, if you don't show your mother this letter, explain to her that your living on me was a matter in which my wishes were not consulted for a moment. It was simply a peculiar, and to me personally most distressing form that your devotion to me took. To make yourself dependent on me for the smallest as well as the largest sums

lent you in your own eyes all the charm of childhood, and in the insisting on my paying for every one of your pleasures you thought that you had found the secret of eternal youth. I confess that it pains me when I hear of your mother's remarks about me, and I am sure that on reflection you will agree with me that if she has no word of regret or sorrow for the ruin your race has brought on mine it would be better if she remained silent. Of course there is no reason she should see any portion of this letter that refers to any mental development I have been going through, or to any point of departure I hope to attain to. It would not be interesting to her. But the parts concerned purely with your life I should show her if I were you.

If I were you, in fact, I would not care about being loved on false pretences. There is no reason why a man should show his life to the world. The world does not understand things. But with people whose affection one desires to have it is different. A great friend of mine – a friend of ten years' standing – came to see me some time ago and told me that he did not believe a single word of what was said against me, and wished me to know that he considered me quite innocent, and the victim of a hideous plot concocted by your Father. I burst into tears at what he said, and told him that while there was much amongst your Father's definite charges that was quite untrue and transferred to me by revolting malice, still that my life had

been full of perverse pleasures and strange passions, and that unless he accepted that fact as a fact about me and realised it to the full, I could not possibly be friends with him any more, or ever be in his company. It was a terrible shock to him, but we are friends, and I have not got his friendship on false pretences. To be forced to tell lies is much worse.

I remember as I was sitting in the dock on the occasion of my last trial listening to Lockwood's appalling denunciation of me – like a thing out of Tacitus, like a passage in Dante, like one of Savonarola's indictments of the Popes at Rome – and being sickened with horror at what I heard. Suddenly it occurred to me, '*How splendid it would be if I was saying all this about myself!*' I saw then at once that what is said of a man is nothing. The point is, who says it. A man's very highest moment is, I have no doubt at all, when he kneels in the dust, and beats his breast, and tells all the sins of his life. So with you. You would be much happier if you let your mother know a little at any rate of your life from yourself. I told her a good deal about it in December 1893, but of course I was forced into reticences and generalities. It did not seem to give her any more courage in her relations with you. On the contrary. She avoided looking at the truth more persistently than ever. If you told her yourself it would be different. My words may perhaps be often too bitter to you, but the facts you cannot deny. Things were as I have said

they were, and if you have read this letter as carefully as you should have done you have met yourself face to face.

I have now written, and at great length, to you in order that you should realise what you were to me before my imprisonment, during those three years' fatal friendship: what you have been to me during my imprisonment, already within two moons of its completion almost: and what I hope to be to myself and to others when my imprisonment is over. I cannot reconstruct my letter, or rewrite it. You must take it as it stands, blotted in many places with tears, in some with the signs of passion or pain, and make it out as best you can, blots, corrections and all. As for the corrections and *errata*, I have made them in order that my words should be an absolute expression of my thoughts, and err neither through surplusage nor through being inadequate. Language requires to be tuned, like a violin: and just as too many or too few vibrations in the voice of the singer or the trembling of the string will make the note false, so too much or too little in words will spoil the message. As it stands, at any rate, my letter has its definite meaning behind every phrase. There is in it nothing of rhetoric. Wherever there is erasion or substitution, however slight, however elaborate, it is because I am seeking to render my real impression, to find for my mood its exact equivalent. Whatever is first in feeling, comes always last in form.

I will admit that it is a severe letter. I have not spared you. Indeed you may say that, after admitting that to weigh

De Profundis

you against the smallest of my sorrows, the meanest of my losses would be really unfair to you, I have actually done so, and made scruple by scruple the most careful assay of your nature. That is true. But you must remember that you put yourself into the scales.

You must remember that, if when matched with one mere moment of my imprisonment the balance in which you lie kicks the beam, Vanity made you choose the balance, and Vanity made you cling to it. *There* was the one great psychological error of our friendship, its entire want of proportion. You forced your way into a life too large for you, one whose orbit transcended your power of vision no less than your power of cyclic motion, one whose thoughts, passions and actions were of intense import, of wide interest, and fraught, too heavily indeed, with wonderful or awful consequence. Your little life of little whims and moods was admirable in its own little sphere. It was admirable at Oxford, where the worst that could happen to you was a reprimand from the Dean or a lecture from the President, and where the highest excitement was Magdalen becoming head of the river, and the lighting of a bonfire in the quad as a celebration of the august event. It should have continued in its own sphere after you left Oxford. In yourself, you were all right. You were a very complete specimen of a very modern type. It was simply in reference to me that you were wrong. Your reckless extravagance was not a crime. Youth is always

extravagant. It was your forcing me to pay for your extravagances that was disgraceful. Your desire to have a friend with whom you could pass your time from morning to night was charming. It was almost idyllic. But the friend you fastened on should not have been a man of letters, an artist, one to whom your continual presence was as utterly destructive of all beautiful work as it was actually paralysing to the creative faculty. There was no harm in your seriously considering that the most perfect way of passing an evening was to have a champagne dinner at the Savoy, a box at a Music-Hall to follow, and a champagne supper at Willis's as a *bonne-bouche* for the end. Heaps of delightful young men in London are of the same opinion. It is not even an eccentricity. It is the qualification for becoming a member of White's. But you had no right to require of me that I should become the purveyor of such pleasures for you. It showed your lack of any real appreciation of my genius. Your quarrel with your Father, again, whatever one may think about its character, should obviously have remained a question entirely between the two of you. It should have been carried on in a backyard. Such quarrels, I believe, usually are. Your mistake was in insisting on its being played as a tragi-comedy on a high stage in History, with the whole world as the audience, and myself as the prize for the victor in the contemptible contest. The fact that your father loathed you, and that you loathed your father, was not a matter of any

interest to the English public. Such feelings are very common in English domestic life, and should be confined to the place they characterise: the home. Away from the home-circle they are quite out of place. To translate them is an offence. Family-life is not to be treated as a red flag to be flaunted in the streets, or a horn to be blown hoarsely on the housetops. You took Domesticity out of its proper sphere, just as you took yourself out of your proper sphere.

And those who quit their proper sphere change their surroundings merely, not their natures. They do not acquire the thoughts or passions appropriate to the sphere they enter. It is not in their power to do so. Emotional forces, as I say somewhere in *Intentions*, are as limited in extent and duration as the forces of physical energy. The little cup that is made to hold so much can hold so much and no more, though all the purple vats of Burgundy be filled with wine to the brim, and the treaders stand knee-deep in the gathered grapes of the stony vineyards of Spain. There is no error more common than that of thinking that those who are the causes or occasions of great tragedies share in the feelings suitable to the tragic mood: no error more fatal than expecting it of them. The martyr in his 'shirt of flame' may be looking on the face of God, but to him who is piling the faggots or loosening the logs for the blast the whole scene is no more than the slaying of an ox is to the butcher, or the felling of a tree to the charcoal burner in the forest, or the fall of a flower to

Oscar Wilde

one who is mowing down the grass with a scythe. Great passions are for the great of soul, and great events can be seen only by those who are on a level with them. I know of nothing in all Drama more incomparable from the point of view of Art, or more suggestive in its subtlety of observation, than Shakespeare's drawing of Rosencrantz and Guildenstern. They are Hamlet's College friends. They have been his companions. They bring with them memories of pleasant days together. At the moment when they come across him in the play he is staggering under the weight of a burden intolerable to one of his temperament. The dead have come armed out of the grave to impose on him a mission at once too great and too mean for him. He is a dreamer, and he is called upon to act. He has the nature of the poet, and he is asked to grapple with the common complexity of cause and effect, with life in its practical realisation, of which he knows nothing, not with life in its ideal essence, of which he knows so much. He has no conception of what to do, and his folly is to feign folly. Brutus used madness as a cloak to conceal the sword of his purpose, the dagger of his will, but to Hamlet madness is a mere mask for the hiding of weakness. In the making of moods and jests he sees a chance of delay. He keeps playing with action, as an artist plays with a theory. He makes himself the spy of his proper actions, and listening to his own words knows them to be but 'words, words, words'. Instead of trying to be the

hero of his own history, he seeks to be the spectator of his own tragedy. He disbelieves in everything, including himself, and yet his doubt helps him not, as it comes not from scepticism but from a divided will. Of all this, Guildenstern and Rosencrantz realise nothing. They bow and smirk and smile, and what the one says the other echoes with sicklier iteration. When at last, by means of the play within the play and the puppets in their dalliance, Hamlet 'catches the conscience' of the King, and drives the wretched man in terror from his throne, Guildenstern and Rosencrantz see no more in his conduct than a rather painful breach of court-etiquette. That is as far as they can attain to in 'the contemplation of the spectacle of life with appropriate Emotions'. They are close to his very secret and know nothing of it. Nor would there be any use in telling them. They are the little cups that can hold so much and no more. Towards the close it is suggested that caught in a cunning spring set for another, they have met, or may meet with a violent and sudden death. But a tragic ending of this kind, though touched by Hamlet's humour with something of the surprise and justice of comedy, is really not for such as they. They never die. Horatio who, in order to 'report Hamlet and his cause aright to the unsatisfied,'

> 'Absents him from felicity a while,
> And in this harsh world draws his breath in pain,'

dies, though not before an audience, and leaves no brother. But Guildenstern and Rosencrantz are as immortal as Angelo and Tartuffe, and should rank with them. They are what modern life has contributed to the antique ideal of friendship. He who writes anew *De Amicitia* must find a niche for them, and praise them in Tusculan prose. They are types fixed for all time. To censure them would show a lack of appreciation. They are merely out of their sphere: that is all. In sublimity of soul there is no contagion. High thoughts and high emotions are by their very existence isolated. What Opheha herself could not understand was not to be realised by 'Guildenstern and gentle Rosencrantz', by 'Rosencrantz and gentle Guildenstern'. Of course I do not propose to compare you. There is a wide difference between you. What with them was chance, with you was choice. Deliberately and by me uninvited you thrust yourself into my sphere, usurped there a place for which you had neither right nor qualifica- tions, and having by curious persistence, and by the rendering of your very presence a part of each separate day, succeeded in absorbing my entire life, could do no better with that life than break it in pieces. Strange as It may sound to you, it was but natural that you should do so. If one gives to a child a toy too wonderful for its little mind, or too beautiful for its but half-awakened eyes, it breaks the toy, if it is wilful, if it is listless it lets it fall and goes its way to its own companions. So it was with you. Having got hold of my

life, you did not know what to do with it. You couldn't have known. It was too wonderful a thing to be in your grasp. You should have let it slip from your hands and gone back to your own companions at their play. But unfortunately you were wilful, and so you broke it. That, when everything is said, is perhaps the ultimate secret of all that has happened. For secrets are always smaller than their manifestations. By the displacement of an atom a world may be shaken. And that I may not spare myself any more than you I will add this: that dangerous to me as my meeting with you was, it was rendered fatal to me by the particular moment in which we met. For you were at that time of life when all that one does is no more than the sowing of the seed, and I was at that time of life when all that one does is no less than the reaping of the harvest.

There are some few things more about which I must write to you. The first is about my Bankruptcy. I heard some days ago, with great disappointment I admit, that it is too late now for your Family to pay your Father off, that it would be illegal, and that I must remain in my present painful position for some considerable time to come. It is bitter to me because I am assured on legal authority that I cannot even publish a book without the permission of the Receiver to whom all the accounts must be submitted. I cannot enter into a contract with the manager of a Theatre, or produce a play without the receipts passing to your Father

and my few other creditors. I think that even you will admit now that the scheme of 'scoring off' your Father by allowing him to make me a bankrupt has not really been the brilliant all round success you imagined it was going to turn out. It has not been so to me at any rate, and my feelings of pain and humiliation at my pauperism should have been consulted rather than your own sense of humour, however caustic or unexpected. In point of actual fact in permitting my Bankruptcy, as in urging me on to the original trial, you really were playing right into your Father's hands, and doing just what he wanted. Alone, and unassisted, he would from the very outset have been powerless. In you – though you did not mean to hold such a horrible office – he has always found his chief ally. I am told by More Adey in his letter that last summer you really did express on more than one occasion your desire to repay me 'a little of what I spent' on you. As I said to him in my answer, unfortunately I spent on you my art, my life, my name, my place in history, and if your family had all the marvellous things in the world at their command, or what the world holds as marvellous, genius, beauty, wealth, high position and the like, and laid them all at my feet, it would not repay me for one tithe of the smallest things that have been taken from me, or one tear of the least tears that I have shed. However, of course everything one does has to be paid for. Even to the Bankrupt it is so. You seem to be under the impression that Bankruptcy

is a convenient means by which a man can avoid paying his debts, a 'score off his creditors' in fact. It is quite the other way. It is the method by which a man's creditors 'score off' him, if we are to continue your favourite phrase, and by which the Law by the confiscation of all his property forces him to pay every one of his debts, and if he fails to do so leaves him as penniless as the commonest mendicant who stands in an archway, or creeps down a road, holding out his hand for the alms for which, in England at any rate, he is afraid to ask. The Law has taken from me not merely all that I have, my books, furniture, pictures, my copyright in my published works, my copyright in my plays, everything in fact from *The Happy Prince* and *Lady Windermere's Fan* down to the stair-carpets and door-scraper of my house, but also all that I am ever going to have. My interest in my marriage-settlement, for instance, was sold. Fortunately I was able to buy it in through my friends. Otherwise, in case my wife died, my two children during my life-time would be as penniless as myself. My interest in our Irish estate, entailed on me by my own Father, will I suppose have to go next. I feel very bitterly about its being sold, but I must submit. Your Father's seven hundred pence, – or pounds is it? – stand in the way, and must be refunded. Even when I am stripped of all I have, and am ever to have, and am granted a discharge as a hopeless Insolvent, I have still got to pay my debts. The Savoy dinners – the clear turtle-soup,

the luscious ortolans wrapped in their crinkled Sicilian vineleaves, the heavy amber-coloured, indeed almost amber-scented champagne – Dagonet 1880, I think, was your favourite wine? – all have still to be paid for. The suppers at Willis', the special *cuvée* of Perrier-Jouet reserved always for us, the wonderful *pâtes* procured directly from Strasburg, the marvellous *fin-champagne* served always at the bottom of great bell-shaped glasses that its bouquet might be the better savoured by the true epicures of what was really exquisite in life – these cannot be left unpaid, as bad debts of a dishonest *client*. Even the dainty sleeve-links – four heart-shaped moonstones of silver mist, girdled by alternate ruby and diamond for their setting – that I designed, and had made at Henry Lewis's as a special little present to you, to celebrate the success of my second comedy, – these even – though I believe you sold them for a song a few months afterwards – have to be paid for. I cannot leave the jeweller out of pocket for the presents I gave you, no matter what you did with them. So, even if I get my discharge, you see I have still my debts to pay. And what is true of a bankrupt is true of everyone else in life. For every single thing that is done someone has to pay. Even you yourself – with all your desire for absolute freedom from all duties, your insistence on having everything supplied to you by others, your attempts to reject any claim on your affection, or regard, or gratitude, – even you will have someday to reflect seriously

on what you have done, and try, however unavailingly, to make some attempt at atonement. The fact that you will not be able really to do so will be part of your punishment. You can't wash your hands of all responsibility, and propose with a shrug or a smile to pass on to a new friend and a freshly spread feast. You can't treat all that you have brought upon me as a sentimental reminiscence to be served up occasionally with the cigarettes and *liqueurs*, a picturesque background to a modern life of pleasure like an old tapestry hung in a common inn. It may for the moment have the charm of a new sauce or a fresh vintage, but the scraps of a banquet grow stale, and the dregs of a bottle are bitter. Either today, or tomorrow, or someday you have got to realise it. Otherwise you may die without having done so, and then what a mean, starved, unimaginative life you would have had. In my letter to More I have suggested one point of view from which you had better approach the subject as soon as possible. He will tell you what it is. To understand it you will have to cultivate your imagination. Remember that imagination is the quality that enables one to see things and people in their real as in their ideal relations. If you cannot realise it by yourself, talk to others on the subject. I have had to look at my past face to face. Look at your past face to face. Sit down quietly and consider it. The supreme vice is shallowness. Whatever is realised is right. Talk to your brother about it. Indeed the proper person to talk to

is Percy. Let him read this letter, and know all the circumstances of our friendship. When things are clearly put before him, no judgment is better. Had we told him the truth, what a lot would have been saved to me of suffering and disgrace! You remember I proposed to do so, the night you arrived in London from Algiers. You absolutely refused. So when he came in after dinner we had to play the comedy of your father being an insane man subject to absurd and unaccountable delusions. It was a capital comedy while it lasted, none the less so because Percy took It all quite seriously. Unfortunately it ended in a very revolting manner. The subject on which I write now is one of its results, and if it be a trouble to you, pray do not forget that it is the deepest of my humiliations, and one I must go through. I have no option. You have none, either.

The second thing about which I have to speak to you is with regard to the conditions, circumstances, and place of our meeting when my term of imprisonment is over. From extracts from your letter to Robbie written in the early summer of last year I understand that you have sealed up in two packages my letters and my presents to you, – such at least as remain of either – and are anxious to hand them personally to me. It is, of course, necessary that they should be given up. You did not understand why I wrote beautiful letters to you, any more than you understood why I gave you beautiful presents. You failed to see that the former were

not meant to be published, any more than the latter were
meant to be pawned. Besides, they belong to a side of life
that is long over, to a friendship that somehow you were
unable to appreciate at its proper value. You must look back
with wonder now to the days when you had my entire life
in your hands. I too look back to them with wonder, and
with other, with far different, emotions.... I am to be released,
if all goes well with me, towards the end of May, and hope
to go at once to some little seaside village abroad with Robbie
and More Adey. The sea, as Euripides says, in one of his
plays about Iphigeneia, washes away the stains and wounds
of the world. θαλασσα κλυζει παντα ταυθρωπων κακα.
I hope to be at least a month with my friends, and to gain,
in their healthful and affectionate company, peace, and
balance, and a less troubled heart, and a sweeter mood. I
have a strange longing for the great simple primeval things,
such as the Sea, to me no less of a mother than the Earth.
It seems to me that we all look at Nature too much, and
live with her too little. I discern great sanity in the Greek
attitude. They never chattered about sunsets, or discussed
whether the shadows on the grass were really mauve or not.
But they saw that the sea was for the swimmer, and the
sand for the feet of the runner. They loved the trees for the
shadow that they cast, and the forest for its silence at noon.
The vineyard-dresser wreathed his hair with ivy that he
might keep off the rays of the sun as he stooped over the

young shoots, and for the artist and the athlete, the two types that Greece gave us, they plaited into garlands the leaves of the bitter laurel and of the wild parsley which else had been of no service to men. We call ourselves a utilitarian age, and we do not know the uses of any single thing. We have forgotten that Water can cleanse, and Fire purify, and that the Earth is mother to us all. As a consequence our Art is of the Moon and plays with shadows, while Greek art is of the Sun and deals directly with things. I feel sure that in elemental forces there is purification, and I want to go back to them and live in their presence.

Of course to one so modern as I am, 'Enfant de mon siècle', merely to look at the world will be always lovely. I tremble with pleasure when I think that on the very day of my leaving prison both the laburnum and the lilac will be blooming in the gardens, and that I shall see the wind stir into restless beauty the swaying gold of the one, and make the other toss the pale purple of its plumes so that all the air shall be Arabia for me. Linnaeus fell on his knees and wept for joy when he saw for the first time the long heath of some English upland made yellow with the tawny aromatic blossoms of the common furze, and I know that for me, to whom flowers are part of desire, there are tears waiting in the petals of some rose. It has always been so with me from my boyhood. There is not a single colour hidden away in the chalice of a flower, or the curve of a

shell, to which, by some subtle sympathy with the very soul of things, my nature does not answer. Like Gautier I have always been one of those *'pour qui le monde visible existe'*. Still, I am conscious now that behind all this Beauty, satisfying though it be, there is some Spirit hidden of which the painted forms and shapes are but modes of manifestation, and it is with this Spirit that I desire to become in harmony. I have grown tired of the articulate utterances of men and things. The Mystical in Art, the Mystical in Life, the Mystical in Nature, – this is what I am looking for, and in the great symphonies of Music, in the initiation of Sorrow, in the depths of the Sea I may find it. It is absolutely necessary for me to find it somewhere. All trials are trials for one's life, just as all sentences are sentences of death, and three times have I been tried. The first time I left the box to be arrested, the second time to be led back to the House of Detention, the third time to pass into a prison for two years. Society, as we have constituted it, will have no place for me, has none to offer; but Nature, whose sweet rains fall on unjust and just alike, will have clefts in the rocks where I may hide, and secret valleys in whose silence I may weep undisturbed. She will hang the night with stars so that I may walk abroad in the darkness without stumbling, and send the wind over my footprints so that none may track me to my hurt: she will cleanse me in great waters, and with bitter herbs make me whole.... At the

end of a month, when the June roses are in all their wanton opulence, I will, if I feel able, arrange through Robbie to meet you in some quiet foreign town like Bruges, whose grey houses and green canals and cool still ways had a charm for me, years ago. For the moment you will have to change your name. The little title of which you were so vain, – and indeed it made your name sound like the name of a flower – you will have to surrender, if you wish to see *me*; just as *my* name, once so musical in the mouth of Fame, will have to be abandoned by me in turn. How narrow, and mean, and inadequate to its burdens is this century of ours! It can give to Success its palace of porphyry, but for Sorrow and Shame it does not keep even a wattled house in which they may dwell: all it can do for *me* is to bid me alter my name into some other name, where even mediaevalism would have given me the cowl of the monk or the face-cloth of the leper behind which I might be at peace…. I hope that our meeting will be what a meeting between you and me should be, after every thing that has occurred. In old days there was always a wide chasm between us, the chasm of achieved Art and acquired culture: there is a still wider chasm between us now, the chasm of Sorrow: but to Humility there is nothing that is impossible, and to Love all things are easy.

As regards your letter to me in answer to this, it may be as long or as short as you choose. Address the envelope

to 'The Governor, H.M. Prison, Reading': inside, in another, and an open envelope, place your own letter to me: if your paper is very thin do not write on both sides, as it makes it hard for others to read. I have written to you with perfect freedom. You can write to me with the same. What I must know from you is why you have never made any attempt to write to me, since the August of the year before last, more especially after, in the May of last year, eleven months ago now, you knew, and admitted to others that you knew, how you had made me suffer, and how I realised it. I waited month after month to hear from you. Even if I had not been waiting, but had shut the doors against you, you should have remembered that no one can possibly shut the doors against Love for ever. The unjust judge in the Gospels rises up at length to give a just decision because Justice comes knocking daily at his door; and at night-time the friend, in whose heart there is no real friendship, yields at length to his friend 'because of his importunity'. There is no prison in any world into which Love cannot force an entrance. If you did not understand that, you did not understand anything about Love at all. Then, let me know all about your article on me for the *Mercure de France*. I know something of it. You had better quote from it. It is set up in type. Also, let me know the exact terms of your Dedication of your poems. If it is in prose, quote the prose; if in verse, quote the verse. I have

no doubt that there will be beauty in it. Write to me with full frankness about yourself: about your life: your friends: your occupations: your books. Tell me about your volume and its reception. Whatever you have to say for yourself, say it without fear. Don't write what you don't mean: that is all. If anything in your letter is false or counterfeit I shall detect it by the ring at once. It is not for nothing, or to no purpose, that in my life-long cult of literature I have made myself

> 'Miser of sound and syllable, no less
> Than Midas of his coinage.'

Remember also that I have yet to know you. Perhaps we have yet to know each other.

For yourself, I have but this last thing to say. Do not be afraid of the past. If people tell you that it is irrevocable, do not believe them. The past, the present and the future are but one moment in the sight of God, in whose sight we should try to live. Time and space, succession and extension, are merely accidental conditions of Thought. The Imagination can transcend them, and move in a free sphere of ideal existences. Things, also, are in their essence what we choose to make them. A thing *is*, according to the mode in which one looks at it. 'Where others', says Blake, 'see but the Dawn coming over the hill, I see the sons of God shouting for joy.'

De Profundis

What seemed to the world and to myself my future I lost irretrievably when I let myself be taunted into taking the action against your Father: had, I dare say, lost it really long before that. What lies before me is my past. I have got to make myself look on that with different eyes, to make the world look on it with different eyes, to make God look on it with different eyes. This I cannot do by ignoring it, or slighting it, or praising it, or denying it. It is only to be done by fully accepting it as an inevitable part of the evolution of my life and character: by bowing my head to everything that I have suffered. How far I am away from the true temper of soul, this letter in its changing, uncertain moods, its scorn and bitterness, its aspirations and its failure to realise those aspirations, shows you quite clearly. But do not forget in what a terrible school I am sitting at my task. And incomplete, imperfect, as I am, yet from me you may have still much to gain. You came to me to learn the Pleasure of Life and the Pleasure of Art. Perhaps I am chosen to teach you something much more wonderful, the meaning of Sorrow, and its beauty.

Your affectionate friend
Oscar Wilde